Praise for *New York Disrupted*

For thirty-five years I claimed Chicago as my ministry lab with studying, networking, preaching, and teaching. It was an enormous privilege. Now, I will confess that every time I went to New York City, it seemed almost as if Chicago was a village by comparison.

On one of my visits to NYC, I read in the *New York Times* that one Flushing, Queens, neighborhood had residents from 133 nations living in it. I recognized that neighborhood as the one where Mac Pier lived. That one New York neighborhood represented *two-thirds* of the world's countries. So imagine my awe as I realized God had given Mac and colleagues the calling of stewarding Kingdom resources, bringing them into relationships, and collaborating for the glory of God in this great city.

Read *New York Disrupted* and be amazed. Better still, use it to take a fresh look at your own city.

—Ray Bakke
Founder, International Urban Associates
Seattle, Washington

What has New York City to do with Athens? Mac Pier narrates the big story of God's movement in New York City, intersecting many shorter stories and distilling out of them many practical principles and guidelines providing inspiration and wisdom that we can apply to Athens and all the great cities of the world.

—Giotis Kantartzis
Pastor, First Greek Evangelical Church;
Coordinator, City to City Balkans, Athens, Greece

In a season of great disruption, this book speaks hope, and heaps of it. Mac Pier is a visionary leader who draws on a lifetime of ministry to outline an inspiring gospel strategy for New York City and, potentially, every city.

—Ian Shelton
Coordinator, Movement Day Australia and South Pacific
Australia

If you believe that prayer has the ability to change a city and you live in a city in need of change, this book will connect the dots.

—Jurie Kriel
Interim CEO, MDDFW; Movement.org
Austin, Texas

Mac is an extraordinary leader with a unique gifting to mobilize and deploy influencers for the good of the city and the glory of God. This book is a must read!

—Nicole Martin
Executive director of Trauma Healing, American Bible Society
Baltimore, Maryland

Mac Pier is one of those rare individuals who combines God-sized dreams, practical realities, and the humility to encourage and promote others to accomplish those dreams. Mac not only tells the Kingdom story of New York City but has lived and shaped it. As you turn the pages, you will find a blueprint for "His" story in your city.

—Rick Rusaw
Coauthor of *Externally Focused Church*; on executive team of Gloo;
cofounder of Spire Network
Boulder, Colorado

Mac Pier calls us to embrace a transgenerational decadal vision of gospel fruitfulness that is fueled by prayer, framed by church planting, and focused on mobilizing the young, empowering the marginalized, and unleashing the marketplace. It is a Kingdom vision for any who are gripped by God's love for cities and desire to see it manifested in their day.

—Claude Alexander
Pastor, Park Church
Charlotte, North Carolina

Mac Pier has written this masterpiece on the past, present, and future of New York City's Christian impact. This book motivates every city leadership team to dream big and plan strategically to bring spiritual, social, and economic revolution in the next ten years. This is a great guide on how we as Christian leaders should utilize the disruption caused by the COVID-19 pandemic to plant churches, mentor youth leaders, transform marginalized communities, and mobilize the marketplace in our cities.

—MARK VISVASAM
Global Hub leader, Movement.org
Chennai, India

Reading a Mac Pier manuscript is like watching a master champion of champions at work—ever inspiring and empowering entrepreneurial and innovative leaders to rethink and reshape tomorrow's church. As a veteran city-movement practitioner, I commend Mac's challenge to those called to shape their city's "Kingdom ecosystem" and to seek our Master Builder for a "decadal" transformational vision for our community. In Mac's view, this vision is anchored not in our best skill sets and strategies, but in the promises of a God who hears and answers the petitions of helplessly disrupted sojourners seeking the welfare of their local communities.

—TOM WHITE
Founder, City Advance; coordinator,
Global Cities Leadership Community
Corvallis, Oregon

No one has a better sense of what it takes to create a movement of God in a city than Mac Pier. His grasp of the global church is unparalleled. In *New York Disrupted,* Mac draws from his vast experience in NYC to project substantive actions that, if taken, can lead to transformation in any city.

—JIM RUNYAN
Board chair emeritus, Movement.org
Dallas, Texas

New York Disrupted is an epic snapshot of a multisector community of faith making a collective impact through unity. Mac Pier's eyewitness account, reflection on New York City history, and pragmatic outline for a decadal vision not only tells NYC's developing story, but provides inspiration and a roadmap for any city catalyst wanting to bear fruit in the way of Christ for the good of their city.

—MARK MATLOCK
Principal, WisdomWorks; author, *Faith for Exiles*
Dallas, Texas

Three things that I know and love about Mac Pier are his spiritual intellect, humility, and contagious passion. He has a global panoramic perspective—an acute awareness of history, an insight into the present context, and a prophetic sense of future possibilities. He has been strategically central to the New York City gospel story over the past thirty years, which is significant as a model of best practices for cities around the world at this important historical juncture of an urbanized world.

—PETER WATT
Lead pastor, (3C) Church
(City Story, Movement Day Africa)
Durban, South Africa

At times, a current reality seems inescapable, especially in a megacity. Mac Pier reveals how past struggles in one of the world's most influential cities reveals that a city's past need not predict its future. This book empowers citizens to own a ten-year vision and strategy that can and will bring unity and healing so that everyone will experience hope and justice.

—JIM LISKE
Director, US Cities, Movement.org
Holland, Michigan

A great addition to the Disruptive series and a tribute to the tenth anniversary of Movement Day. Building on New York City's unique history, people, and stories, Mac develops models and strategies toward a compelling vision for 2030, exciting and inspiring for all city leaders who want to see their cities moving into their destiny.

—NATALIE CHAN
Director, Ray Bakke Centre for Urban Transformation,
Bethel Bible Seminary
Hong Kong

After more than twenty years in ministry, I have never met a person like Mac who is always so passionate to talk about unity and collaboration of the body of Christ to see the city transformed. Whoever reads this book will be inspired and motivated to build a unity and collaboration movement for their city with God through tireless prayer.

—ANTON TARIGAN
Lead pastor, Tower of Prayer Church
Jakarta, Indonesia

In this new book, Mac Pier again brings us stories and ideas of real impact and change in the city, formulating a vocabulary, vision, and theology for city gospel movements. His emphasis on prayer; unity across church, marketplace, and nonprofit; and investment in the next generation are core values I have learned from and stand behind.

—LUKE GREENWOOD
European director, Steiger International
Krakow, Poland

New York Disrupted is what Jim Collins would call a BHAG—a Big Hairy Audacious Goal. Over the twenty years that I have known Mac, he has never been short on ideas and passion to see real gospel-empowered change take place. One phrase he uses in his book is the need for *tenacious unity*, and I know he speaks from his heart and from experience because I have seen him live this principle firsthand. This book has the potential to be a rallying cry for church city movements. I can't wait to see what God will do through it.

—STEVEN TOMLINSON
Senior pastor, Shelter Rock Church
Long Island, New York

The New York City story encompasses the core foundations for change and Kingdom renewal: unity, prayer, marketplace leaders, church planting, strategic planning, and outrageous steps of faith. Mac Pier has lived this God story with many others, and documents for us how God is at work in New York City today.

If you feel deeply for your city, if your heart is moved by the plight of the lost and the least, then you need to read this book and find wisdom of how to channel your passion into Kingdom action.

—ROGER SUTTON
Gather, Movement Day UK
Manchester, Great Britain

Mac Pier invites us on a journey into the past to position us for greater Kingdom impact in our future. If you love your city, this is a book to read!

—ANNETTE H. CUTINO
Director, Advance, LEAD.NYC, Movement.org; associate pastor,
Harvest Fields Community Church
New York City, New York

Proverbs 29:18 says, "Where there is no vision, the people perish" (KJV). Mac Pier offers a God-sized vision for what decadal transformation can look like in your city, as you draw upon the leadership example of so many great stewards of vision. Mac is a trailblazer and has written an extraordinary literary work that every city leader should use to actualize gospel movement in the city. Now is the time!

—EBONY S. SMALL
Vice president, Multiplication; PULSE
New York City, New York

This book is a powerful chronicle of New York City. It is history filled with God-stories of how the gospel and His servants have turned the city upside down. There is none other than Mac Pier who can tell this story so powerfully!

—BONNY ANDREWS
Chief dreamer, Transform Cities & LiveJam
New York City, New York

New York Disrupted is a must read for every visionary leader who wants to impact their sphere for the next decade and beyond. Mac Pier shows how God has moved powerfully in the past using crisis to bring revival, how He's moving in our present day through viable ministry and marketplace leaders from Boomers to Gen Z using cutting-edge principles, systems, and trends that have catapulted the gospel from the inner cities to the four corners of the globe. For such a time as this!

—MULLERY JEAN PIERRE
Senior pastor, Beraca Baptist Church
Brooklyn, New York

This book is a must read if you want to understand the heart, mind, and soul of the city.

I have known Mac Pier for more than thirty years and consider it a privilege and an honor to be his friend and copartner in the gospel. He has been a strong, humble leader and visionary who has been the catalyst for unifying pastors and leaders in New York City, the nation, and around the world.

—TOM MAHAIRAS
Founder and president of CitiVision;
pastor emeritus of Manhattan Bible Church
New York City, New York

A leading ministry strategist has produced a concise encyclopedia on the evangelicals in New York City and a roadmap to their future.

—TONY CARNES
Publisher and editor, *A Journey through NYC Religions*
New York City, New York

This fast-paced book is for every leader in every city! Using the story and vision of NYC, Mac Pier soon has you dreaming about your city and wondering, *What could a decade of fruitful effort look like?* With inspiration from *New York Disrupted*, put action toward your city's "North Star."

—CRAIG SIDER
President and CEO, Movement.org
Philadelphia, Pennsylvania

The passion and vision Mac has for gospel movements in cities comes through clearly in this book. I hope many more leaders in cities around the world will hear his clarion call and rise up to join this powerful move of God for the completion of world evangelization!

—JONATHAN WONG
Pastor, Church of the Good Shepherd (English)
Singapore

In *New York Disrupted*, Mac Pier draws us into one of the most compelling city stories of our generation. With his masterful storytelling and keen insights, Mac uncovers the key principles that can help leaders chart a hopeful path to see global cities transformed in the coming decade.

—TIM DAY
Executive director, City Movement Canada
Toronto, Ontario, Canada

Mac Pier has done the Christians in New York City a great service by exploring how the historical context of the city impacts the current beliefs of New Yorkers and the structures and institutions in which they operate. I truly believe *New York Disrupted* will provide a biblical platform for future Kingdom work—not only in New York City, but around the world.

—MARK HARRIS
Founder, 4Tucson
Tucson, Arizona

NEW YORK
DISRUPTED

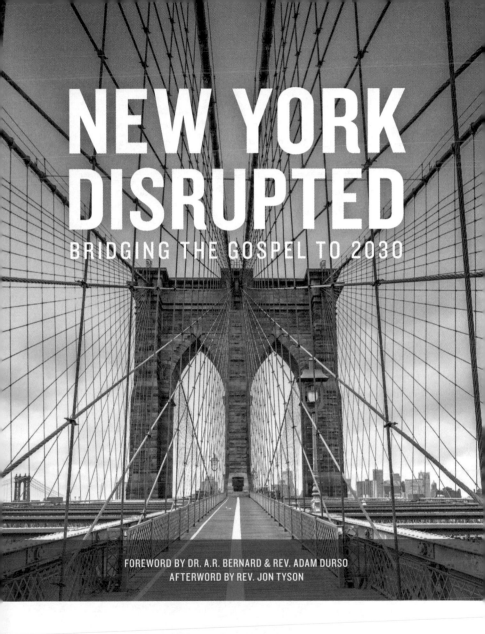

NEW YORK
DISRUPTED

BRIDGING THE GOSPEL TO 2030

FOREWORD BY DR. A.R. BERNARD & REV. ADAM DURSO
AFTERWORD BY REV. JON TYSON

MAC PIER

Movement Day Publishing
New York City

Movement Day Publishing is the publishing ministry of Movement.org, an organization that catalyzes leaders in more than two hundred cities to see their cities flourish spiritually and socially. Movement.org trains leaders globally to create their own Movement Day Expressions. For more information, visit movement.org.

New York Disrupted: Bridging the Gospel to 2030
© 2020 by Mac Pier
A Movement Day resource published in alliance with Movement.org.

Edited by Ginger Kolbaba
Interior design by Katherine Lloyd at theDESKonline.com
Cover design by Mattera Management

Cataloging-in-Publication Data is available

ISBN: 978-1-7324353-0-8 (print)
ISBN: 978-1-7324353-4-6 (ebook)
ISBN: 978-1-7324353-5-3 (audio book)

Printed in United States of America

20 21 22 23 24 25 5 4 3 2 1

This book is dedicated to Ed Morgan, Al Miyashita, Larry Christensen, Dave Jennings, Jennifer Depner, and Craig Sider. Thank you for your decades of friendship in the gospel and efforts to launch this decadal vision for New York City.

To Noah, Layla, Hayley, Gabriel, and Lily. May you grow into resilient disciples of Jesus.

CONTENTS

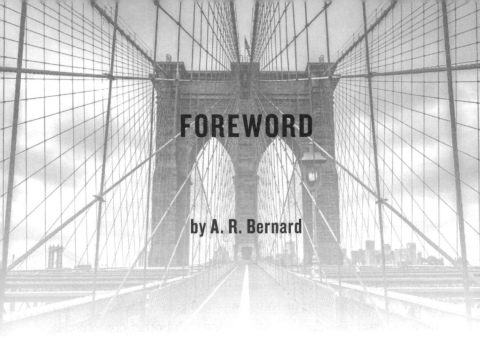

FOREWORD

by A. R. Bernard

The Bible begins in a garden and ends in a city. These are the words of Ray Bakke, one of the fathers of "urban ministry."

The city of God that John the revelator spoke of descends from heaven, remedying all the ills of human existence. It appears, however, after a climactic clash of nations shaped by political, economic, and religious influences.

And the city of Enoch, named after the son of Cain, is the first city mentioned in Scripture: "Cain built a city . . ." Genesis 4:17 (AMP). According to the biblical record, it quickly became a center for the development of housing, ranching, music and entertainment, education, mining, metallurgy, and manufacturing.

I speak of cities because a study of human civilization is a study of the urban experience. The majority of things by which we measure civilization, such as education, art, culture, science, government, social engineering, industry, and religion took place in cities. "Therefore," writes Samuel P. Huntington in *Clash of Civilizations*, "a study of civilization is really a study of 'urban history.'"

Cities are places where more efficient and effective means for the production and distribution of goods and services develop. Cities are also the home of the public square, where the sharing of philosophies, beliefs, values, and ideas that shape the culture take place.

From the cities of ancient Mesopotamia to the Acropolis of Athens, to the cities of Rome, Paris, London, New York, cities have shaped not only industry but cultural norms, traditions, and practices. Cities have birthed terms like *urban, suburban, metropolitan, micropolitan, urban sprawl* in order to understand geographies and patterns of growth, cohesion, and disintegration. Even residents in surrounding rural areas depend on cities for jobs, essential services, public goods, and other commercial and recreational amenities.

Cities are also the breeding ground for social problems, issues of public and private education, economics, employment, healthcare, crime, special interests, and the list goes on.

What fertile ground for the work of the church! Mac Pier understands that the church is more than a religious institution; it is a social-cultural institution, mandated to be not only a prophetic, moral, redemptive, and humanitarian voice but filled with prophetic, moral, redemptive, and humanitarian "activists."

Since 1950, the world's urban population has grown from 746 million to 3.9 billion people. According to the United Nations Department of Economic and Social Affairs, the world's "urban" population will grow to 6.4 billion people by 2050.

These realities present a serious demand for a theology of the city and a strategy for the city.

Mac Pier presents just that—a theology rooted in the biblical belief in the life, dignity, and worth of each person; an understanding of the church's responsibility for the common good; and the gospel of Jesus Christ as the only answer, spiritually and socially, to the ills of fallen humanity.

Change is not an event. Change is a process, sometimes a long-term process requiring a long-term vision and strategy. Mac casts a vision for the future that calls on the power of collective effort. Bringing together those with various areas of expertise and seeking best practices, *New York Disrupted* presents a clear and effective agenda for the church in the city.

Dismissing the bifurcation of church and state presented by the culture, Mac understands that the sacred and the secular are different but connected. By combining the power of the church and the power of the marketplace, God's love, life, and light come alive through the work of the ministry.

COVID-19 and the senseless murder of a black man, George Floyd, by a white police officer in Minnesota created an environment for anger and frustration to be unleashed in ways reminiscent of the civil unrest of the 1960s. But with a major difference. For the first time in American history, a national consensus of moral outrage rose, which included people across the political spectrum, all races and ethnicities, and all sectors of society. It caused a ground swell of support for change.

These are all prophetic indicators that emanate from the character of the culture. A signal to the church that we must not ignore but must strategically respond to.

The anger and frustration are the initial reactions to perceived injustice. But we know that anger is not a call to action. It is a call to prayer that guides our actions. It is therefore providential that the entire strategy of *New York Disrupted* is undergirded by prayer.

If we want to see gospel change in our cities, it's going to take more than one leader or one organization to bring it about.

It's going to take all leaders and all organizations doing their parts. It's going to take training, development, deployment, and ongoing support.

The possibilities for meaningful change lie ahead of us. Let's not miss the opportunity!

—A. R. Bernard
pastor, Christian Cultural Center
founder, New School for Biblical Theology
member, New York Commission of Religious Leaders

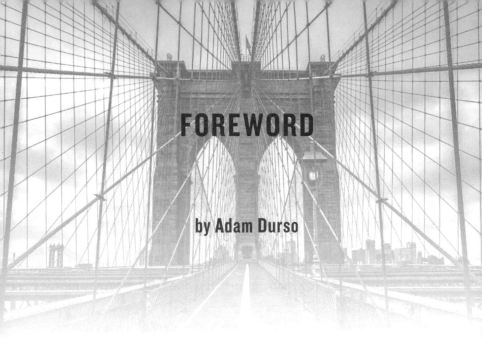

FOREWORD

by Adam Durso

I have had the privilege of knowing Dr. McKenzie Pier (AKA Mac) for more than twenty years. His commitment to a biblical framework for leadership has fathered a thirty-year prayer movement and seeded the most influential leadership network in New York City.

As you journey through this book, you will read both the historical context of how God uses disruption to establish His Kingdom and stories from practitioners who are serving communities, changing lives, and catalyzing change here every single day.

Now, put on your "futuring" lenses and get ready to contemplate this question: "Are you ready for an NYC where . . .?"

Are you ready for an NYC where churches are planted by the hundreds to reach the unchurched, disciple believers, and model incarnational ministry over the next ten years? These newer churches would be mentored by existing, more mature, and seasoned church leaders fathering an intergenerational climate of leadership. We would model for the world partnership and collaboration instead of competition, spreading the very fragrance of unity.

Sustainable church planting is not just counting the number of churches planted in a city, but how many of them are still thriving five and ten years later. These pastors will be healthy, leading in community, because they have learned that a leader who has no place to be vulnerable will eventually implode. May NYC in 2030 be a place where leaders commit to pray together, build trust, and have the tough conversations across racial, ethnic, cultural, and denominational lines. Could this be a city where we live up to the mantra "melting pot" and display unity within diversity?

Are you ready for an NYC where a new paradigm is created that doesn't look at Millennials and Generation Z as just the *next* generations, but the *now* generations? Not just the future, but the present and the future. Not just creating younger followers, but empowering these passionate young leaders to lead.

What if in 2030 the fashion, finance, and culture capital of the world is shaped by a younger generation ignited with passion for the living God? A generation who is reached and included and who find their voice through the church of Jesus Christ. Could NYC be the place where generations lead together boldly? Could we have a younger generation emerge while standing on the shoulders of great leaders who have gone before many of us and paved the way? What if the next generation isn't compelled to leave the church, but to find their voice and purpose in the great call of the gospel?

Are you ready for an NYC where the marginalized are served by those who have more because they are driven by their heart for God? An NYC where the chasm that exists between the haves and the have-nots is bridged by the body of Christ, because serving the poor and disenfranchised is not simply a humanitarian thing to do, but a mandate from God.

In our 10 Zip Codes Project research, we examined two of the most fragile neighborhoods in NYC and the impact local Christian churches and nonprofit organizations have as they serve the marginalized. As we extrapolated the data and applied it across the five boroughs, we found that the church is meeting needs at an annual value of more than $8 billion!

What if in 2030 the church is known for using the megaphone that is NYC to give a voice to the voiceless and to speak out against injustice? May this be the place where the most fragile zip codes thrive because of the full gospel of Jesus Christ.

The explosive power of word *and* deed, faith *and* action! Not just "be blessed" but be empowered!

Are you ready for an NYC where the marketplace community is passionate about using their secular influence to catalyze Kingdom advancement? What if in 2030 this passionate group of industry icons were committed to lean in to coach and mentor ministry leaders?

A community of Christian marketplace leaders committed to ethical practices and accountability influencing the economic systems that shape the globe. Men and women who are not consumed with more (more homes, more boats, more cars, more vacations) but with city gospel movements. Wall Street's new "G" word would be *generosity* and not *greed*.

If your answer to these questions is yes, then join me—join the movement.

I am ready for an NYC where churches are planted to look like the communities they belong to while pastors build strong, long-lasting relationships in diverse community.

I am ready for an NYC where the next generation is reached and empowered and finds their voice not outside the church, but right in the heart of it.

I am ready for an NYC where the marginalized are not only served, but the fragile places are strengthened by the underpinnings of the full gospel, and systemic issues of injustice are broken by that same gospel.

I am ready for an NYC where the Christian marketplace leaders of the most influential city on the planet use their secular prestige to see another Kingdom advance—thy Kingdom come, thy will be done on earth and in NYC as it is in heaven.

That's New York disrupted!

—Adam Durso
Executive director, LEAD.NYC

FRUITFULNESS

O n September 11, 2001, 3000 lives were lost when the twin towers of the World Trade Center collapsed, causing the single largest loss of life on any day in American history. Just as its people were picking themselves back up and dusting off from the tragedy, catastrophe stuck again in 2008. The stock market fell, and the country entered an economic recession. While the nation as a whole lost 2.6 million jobs in the aftermath,[1] New York City bore almost 8 percent of the nation's loss when it watched 200,000 private sector jobs disappear.[2]

And yet amid the trauma of the decade, from 2000 to 2009, God was at work in powerful ways. In 2003, the New York City Leadership Center (NYCLC), now called Movement.org, along with Redeemer City to City (CTC), founded by Tim Keller, co-created the Church Multiplication Alliance (CMA); its purpose was to start new churches in New York City to impact thousands of more lives with the gospel.

For the next six years, CMA leaders gathered influencers in the hundreds to hear a vision for new churches renewing New York City. In 2009, CTC and NYCLC leadership co-commissioned the Values Research Institute to study and evaluate to measure the progress of Manhattan church planting. The results stunned and amazed. According to the report, from 1989 to 2009, evangelical Christianity grew by 300 percent (from 1 percent to 3 percent). That meant approximately 30,000 more people were attending churches in Manhattan than were in 1989.[3]

The NYCLC and CTC teams reviewed that research. We decided to establish a gathering one day a year to convene faith-based and civic leaders from the same city or from multiple cities. On that day, we celebrate what God is doing in a city, we co-create a plan to address the city's greatest challenges, and we catalyze action toward a decadal vision—a goal we set to see God move remarkably and measurably in our city toward a

Manhattan Center City Evangelical Churches 2009

197 churches
1 church / 5,853 residents
Church founding

Before 1949	25%
1950-1977	15%
1978-1999	19%
2000-2009	39%

info@valuesresearchinstitute.org

greater destiny for the multitudes of our city. The name of the gathering? Movement Day.

The following year, the first Movement Day took place. The leadership team's aspiration was to have a gathering of New

York City leaders with a few international guests. But on that September 10, 2010, day, 800 leaders arrived from thirty-four states and fourteen countries to listen in on what was happening in New York City.

Now a decade later, more than 40,000 leaders from 400 cities have participated in a Movement Day Expression—from New York City to Dallas, Pretoria to Port-au-Prince. Leaders in cities across six continents are pursuing expressions for their own cities. All within just one decade.

So the question becomes, if God can do this amazing work in ten years, what does He have planned for the next decade? What is a possible destiny for your city and its citizens?

Leading Toward a 2030 Vision

The start of this new decade continues the chaos and trauma of the previous decade, as we faced a global COVID-19 pandemic in which, at the time of this writing, almost 650,000 people died, while millions were infected.[4] And the jobless rate within the United States equaled the numbers seen only during the Great Depression.[5] What does the next ten years look like? We are surrounded by overwhelming needs locally and globally. How should we live and express our leadership in this decade? What should be our organizing principles?

In *Center Church,* Tim Keller, perhaps the most influential global voice on the theme of the gospel in the city, poses this premise: "As I read, reflected, and taught, I came to the conclusion that a more biblical theme for ministerial evaluation than either success or faithfulness is *fruitfulness.*"[6] He embodies what he preaches: Keller and the City to City network have planted more than 400 congregations in global cities.

As we dive into the pages of this book and we consider Keller's thought-provoking and challenging statement, our goal is to answer this question: How can we as a community of leaders be maximally fruitful over the next decade in our respective cities and churches? We want to address this question by focusing on Metro New York City leaders, city leaders globally, and followers of Jesus in any local context.

In 1987, Tim Keller and I began a conversation about fruitfulness. At the time he was researching Manhattan to plant Redeemer Presbyterian Church. For thirty years we have continued the discussion on how to grow evangelical Christianity in Manhattan from 1 percent to 10 percent in our lifetimes. As we stood on the roof of the CTC offices in 2011 to film a video to engage leaders in The New York City Movement Project, Keller declared, "We have a goal. We want to see 10 percent of Manhattan residents attending Bible-believing churches in our lifetime. We may not see it happen, but someday somebody will."[7] Imagine with the eye of faith how *your* city could change if you saw a 100 percent growth in the church community, with vibrant new churches.

As Keller and I continued in our vision-casting discussion, in 2010, we both met with Bob Doll, the chief equity strategist for Nuveen Securities in Cape Town, South Africa, at the Third Lausanne Congress. Doll is one of the most visible and highly respected marketplace Christians in the world, with a weekly newsletter following of 225,000. As we talked, we discovered we all shared the same passion. Keller and I enlisted Doll to join our "three-legged stool" for Movement Day—a pastor (Keller), a marketplace leader (Doll), and a missionary (me). Doll's involvement over the past decade, alongside Keller's teaching, became the greatest success factors in scaling Movement Day. Soon Doll and his wife, Leslie, became lead investors in The

New York City Movement Project and attracted other senior marketplace leaders to engage with Movement Day's strategic acumen, cultural influence, and philanthropy.

In addition, over the past eight years, I've engaged with a group of New York City ministry colleagues who share that vision: Ed Morgan, chairman emeritus of The Bowery Mission; Al Miyashita, associate field director of The Navigators; Larry Christensen, leadership network director for Cru; Dave Jennings, chief operating officer of Nyack College; Craig Sider, chief executive officer of Movement.org; and Jennifer Depner, director of the office of CEO of Movement.org.

We believe that strategic collaboration is a catalyst to strategic fruitfulness. We create exponentially more impact when we work together. To that end, we organized a small entity called Co-Lab, with a goal to create collaborative working space for dozens of faith-based mission agencies in New York City. Co-Lab agencies, of which Movement.org is a member, share space on the seventeenth floor of Nyack College in downtown Manhattan. This team has overseen four working groups, which we will study more closely throughout this book.

Joshua Crossman, CEO and director of Pinetops Foundation, a faith-based foundation that provides grants to strategic faith-based initiatives, has also looked at the power of fruitfulness in our work. In 2018, he wrote a report titled *The Great Opportunity*, the best analysis on the American church in the past fifty years that I am aware of. Crossman makes the compelling argument that unless something dramatic happens in the United States, 50 percent of all American churches will disappear by the year 2050.[8] In his talk at Movement Day in October 2019, Crossman said, "We are five minutes until midnight. We need to act with a profound sense of urgency." He raises a motivating challenge to faith leaders everywhere, but particularly in metropolitan areas such as New York.

From Keller to Co-Lab to Crossman, all raise insight and challenge us to consider the work we do, the impact we can have, and the urgency with which God is calling us to act.

A Roadmap to Decadal Fruitfulness

What will be required for you to create noticeable, lasting impact in your city, community, or church within the next decade? After living in New York City for thirty-five years as both a student and a resident, I have realized five principles that will help us from 2020 to 2030 to give us the kind of fruitfulness we long to see.

Principle #1: To Love Your City, You Must Know Your City

In my analysis in more than thirty city contexts globally, I have found that the average leader in the average church has little idea of the realities of their own city. Few leaders understand the macrotrends in their cities regarding demography, socio-economics, church population, and other important trends. Why does that matter? Because people can love only that which they know. The more we know about our past, the more we will care about our future. Good research compels action.

Every movement needs a "North Star"—a vision that represents what a decade of fruitful effort will look like. In 2009, the NYCLC declared our commitment with City to City to plant 100 new Manhattan churches, train 20,000 leaders, and establish Movement Day in 2010. By 2016, just seven years later, the first sixty churches had been planted, 26,000 leaders had been trained, and leaders from 400 cities had participated in

Movement Day. This was all birthed from the 2009 research. Research matters. Measurement matters. If you want to impact your city or community, invest the time to get to know it.

Principle #2: The Church Needs Tenacious Unity

What is a gospel movement? A gospel movement takes place when the growth of Christianity increases faster than the general population, when we see measurable progress against social challenges, and when Christian leaders find their way into positions of cultural influence. What precedes a gospel movement? A community of leaders, agencies, and churches. What precedes the formation of this community? Unity. But not just any kind of unity—not the feel-good, kumbaya unity that we sing around our campfires at church camp. It's a tenacious unity.

By tenacious unity, we mean the kind of unity Paul wrote in Ephesians 4:3, to "make *every effort* to keep the unity of the Spirit through the bond of peace" (emphasis added). To promote unity in the first century, Paul raised money from Gentile Christians to support the Jewish Christian community in Jerusalem.

But why is tenacious unity necessary for the transformation of a community and ultimately for a gospel movement? Because the unity of the church expressing itself in mission needs to be the driver behind everything else we do in public witness. The unity of the church was foremost on Jesus' mind less than twenty-four hours before He died as He prayed His extraordinary prayer in John 17. Jesus linked the themes of God's glory and our mission to the theme of our unity in Him.

Division in the church breeds atheism in the world. The unity of the church breathes the aroma of belief. A united church is the most powerful apologetic toward a believable gospel. Our unity transcends our ethnicity, our geography, our gender, and our generation. Effective leaders are willing to live and die on the hill of visible unity in their city. That's not soft-talking unity; that's a unity that requires tenacity.

Tenacious unity fosters the necessary agreement between leaders to achieve remarkable results, because we *fight* for unity. Jesus had a high view of agreement. He said that when two or three agree in His name, they can do anything (Matthew 18:19). For us, if we want to see a gospel movement in our lifetimes in our cities and communities, then we must agree together, we must seek tenacious unity.

In *Center Church*, Tim Keller writes about that requirement: "Corporate gospel renewal—what has sometimes been called 'revival'—is a season in which a whole body of believers experience personal gospel renewal together. . . . Movements are characterized by a stance of generous flexibility toward other organizations."[9] In order to "be together" in the gospel, we need to be generous toward others of different church cultures. We need to prioritize our unity with other Christians who are different ethnically and denominationally. Our unity is more important than our unique cultural expression of the gospel.

Principle #3: Prayer Is Not an Option

The history of revival in the Bible and in the modern era has taught us that whenever God gets ready to do something, He sets His people to pray together. (We will study this more in-depth in chapter 8.) One of the great truths of the Bible is that several Old Testament pray-ers (Nehemiah, Hannah, and Solomon) teach us that God gave His people the very words to pray.

In 1 Samuel 1, we read that Hannah longed for a son. God needed a leader to guide the nation. Hannah prayed that God would remember her by giving her a son and she vowed to give him back to the Lord all the days of his life. First Samuel 1:19 says that "the LORD remembered her." He responded specifically to the requests she made. This suggests that the great act of praying is initiated by God. He invites us into the cosmic mystery of how He works in the world in personal and corporate prayer.

Principle #4: Strategic Collaboration Will Result in Greater Fruitfulness

Collaboration is the pragmatic expression of unity. When Keller and I started working together in 2003, we married CTC's expertise in church planting with our expertise in convening diverse stakeholders together. The result showed itself in the passion and synergy that thousands of leaders received as they were drawn into a compelling idea that was well executed. As you consider what it means to be more fruitful in your context, marrying your vision to the visions of others will create collaborative fruitfulness.

Principle #5: We Need to Start First with Family Foundations

If we want our cities to experience the reality of the gospel, we need to start with ourselves and our families. We want what we discuss publicly to be true of us privately. As a grandfather of five, I am more convinced than ever that we must live out the values of the gospel in our homes, for it is there that we are called to model faithfulness, sacrifice, generosity, and forgiveness. The greatest crisis facing our homes in cities and culture is fatherlessness. We need to be effective fathers and mothers to our children and grandchildren. Where fatherlessness is rampant, the church, and especially men, must step into that void for the next generation.

The Gospel Ecosystem:
Where Your Leadership Fits in God's Plan

We all want our lives and leadership to matter. As we look to practicing tenacious unity, we remember that we are all members of the body of Christ in our cities with unique abilities and contributions to make. As diverse as we are, we have a main goal—to share the gospel and transform our cities for Christ. This is what Tim Keller calls a gospel ecosystem. In his final chapter of *Center Church,* Keller writes about the gospel ecosystem (see chart below) in which he explains that the basic idea of a gospel ecosystem (GES) is that every city has a group of churches, agencies, and marketplace leaders that are all committed to the gospel in word and deed. This is an ecosystem.[10]

Why is this important for us? This matters because the vibrancy of the gospel in our cities is in proportion to the depth of our unity. More people will come to faith in Jesus when we express our unity as He prayed and as we live out that prayer.

The GES as diagrammed represents three concentric circles:

- **Contextualized theological vision.** The gospel needs to make sense in the context in which it is being presented. For example, I lived in a very international New York City neighborhood for thirty years. The gospel in our context had an extraordinarily strong emphasis on the unity of the church to bridge deep cultural and socioeconomic divides. Our church, First Baptist of Flushing, spoke sixty languages and was made up of forty different denominational backgrounds. What held us together was understanding that we were one new body in Jesus. We *all* need to understand the context in which we live and how we express the gospel relevantly to our neighbors.

- **Church planting and renewal movements.** If Christianity is to grow, it will require the birth of new churches. According to research, churches that are ten years and younger are six to eight times more effective in reaching new people than churches that are older than ten years.[11] This is an opportunity for churches to explore ways for their own renewal as well as ways to assist other churches to get started.

- **Specialized ministries.** These are ministries represented by a community of churches, agencies, leaders, and initiatives.[12]

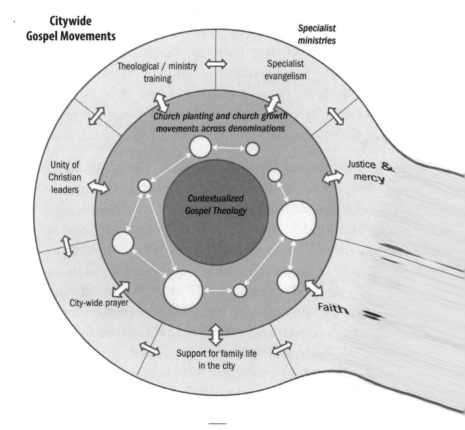

The Gospel Ecosystem:
Where Your Leadership Fits in God's Plan

We all want our lives and leadership to matter. As we look to practicing tenacious unity, we remember that we are all members of the body of Christ in our cities with unique abilities and contributions to make. As diverse as we are, we have a main goal—to share the gospel and transform our cities for Christ. This is what Tim Keller calls a gospel ecosystem. In his final chapter of *Center Church,* Keller writes about the gospel ecosystem (see chart below) in which he explains that the basic idea of a gospel ecosystem (GES) is that every city has a group of churches, agencies, and marketplace leaders that are all committed to the gospel in word and deed. This is an ecosystem.[10]

Why is this important for us? This matters because the vibrancy of the gospel in our cities is in proportion to the depth of our unity. More people will come to faith in Jesus when we express our unity as He prayed and as we live out that prayer.

The GES as diagrammed represents three concentric circles:

- **Contextualized theological vision.** The gospel needs to make sense in the context in which it is being presented. For example, I lived in a very international New York City neighborhood for thirty years. The gospel in our context had an extraordinarily strong emphasis on the unity of the church to bridge deep cultural and socioeconomic divides. Our church, First Baptist of Flushing, spoke sixty languages and was made up of forty different denominational backgrounds. What held us together was understanding that we were one new body in Jesus. We *all* need to understand the context in which we live and how we express the gospel relevantly to our neighbors.

- **Church planting and renewal movements.** If Christianity is to grow, it will require the birth of new churches. According to research, churches that are ten years and younger are six to eight times more effective in reaching new people than churches that are older than ten years.[11] This is an opportunity for churches to explore ways for their own renewal as well as ways to assist other churches to get started.
- **Specialized ministries.** These are ministries represented by a community of churches, agencies, leaders, and initiatives.[12]

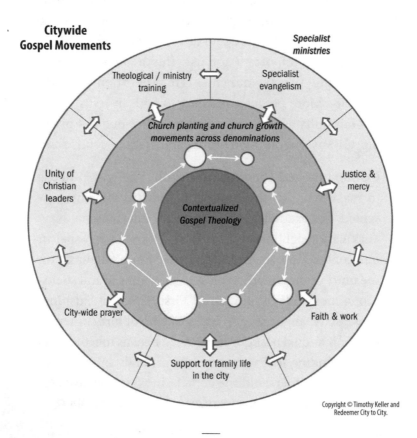

Copyright © Timothy Keller and
Redeemer City to City.

is the most powerful apologetic toward a believable gospel. Our unity transcends our ethnicity, our geography, our gender, and our generation. Effective leaders are willing to live and die on the hill of visible unity in their city. That's not soft-talking unity; that's a unity that requires tenacity.

Tenacious unity fosters the necessary agreement between leaders to achieve remarkable results, because we *fight* for unity. Jesus had a high view of agreement. He said that when two or three agree in His name, they can do anything (Matthew 18:19). For us, if we want to see a gospel movement in our lifetimes in our cities and communities, then we must agree together, we must seek tenacious unity.

In *Center Church*, Tim Keller writes about that requirement: "Corporate gospel renewal—what has sometimes been called 'revival'—is a season in which a whole body of believers experience personal gospel renewal together. . . . Movements are characterized by a stance of generous flexibility toward other organizations."[9] In order to "be together" in the gospel, we need to be generous toward others of different church cultures. We need to prioritize our unity with other Christians who are different ethnically and denominationally. Our unity is more important than our unique cultural expression of the gospel.

Principle #3: Prayer Is Not an Option

The history of revival in the Bible and in the modern era has taught us that whenever God gets ready to do something, He sets His people to pray together. (We will study this more in-depth in chapter 8.) One of the great truths of the Bible is that several Old Testament pray-ers (Nehemiah, Hannah, and Solomon) teach us that God gave His people the very words to pray.

In 1 Samuel 1, we read that Hannah longed for a son. God needed a leader to guide the nation. Hannah prayed that God would remember her by giving her a son and she vowed to give him back to the Lord all the days of his life. First Samuel 1:19 says that "the LORD remembered her." He responded specifically to the requests she made. This suggests that the great act of praying is initiated by God. He invites us into the cosmic mystery of how He works in the world in personal and corporate prayer.

Principle #4: Strategic Collaboration Will Result in Greater Fruitfulness

Collaboration is the pragmatic expression of unity. When Keller and I started working together in 2003, we married CTC's expertise in church planting with our expertise in convening diverse stakeholders together. The result showed itself in the passion and synergy that thousands of leaders received as they were drawn into a compelling idea that was well executed. As you consider what it means to be more fruitful in your context, marrying your vision to the visions of others will create collaborative fruitfulness.

Principle #5: We Need to Start First with Family Foundations

If we want our cities to experience the reality of the gospel, we need to start with ourselves and our families. We want what we discuss publicly to be true of us privately. As a grandfather of five, I am more convinced than ever that we must live out the values of the gospel in our homes, for it is there that we are called to model faithfulness, sacrifice, generosity, and forgiveness. The greatest crisis facing our homes in cities and culture is fatherlessness. We need to be effective fathers and mothers to our children and grandchildren. Where fatherlessness is rampant, the church, and especially men, must step into that void for the next generation.

So what is the point? Why do we need to know about gospel ecosystems? Because the impact of the gospel in a city is in proportion to the depth of unity between diverse members of the same ecosystem. We all need to see ourselves in the GES of our own city and understand where we fit. We need to do everything in our power to enlist other leaders, churches, and agencies to meaningfully participate in the GES of our cities with us. To help make this idea come alive, in the following pages we will look at a case study of how the GES of Metro New York City is working together to grow the impact of the gospel toward a 2030 vision for our region. The hope is that as you read this case study, you will consider what this could look like for your own church, community, and city over the course of a decade.

Make This Next Decade Count

As we journey through this book considering how we can make an impact in our city, community, and church, we must remember that *everything* is rooted in the gospel. In the gospel we see that Jesus came to live the life we should live, He came to die the death we deserve, and in His death, He put death to death. Our entire orientation is to see the gospel go deeper in our lives, to grow in our churches, and to take root in the lives of others in our cities.

Tim Keller's vision is to see at least 10 percent of Manhattan's residents become believers. That is a big goal. But we serve a big God. And He is calling us to step forward, to move heaven and earth, and to make this next decade count.

You have an important role to play. Eternity hangs in the balance. Every person matters. Every life is sacred. Everyone is an image bearer of the *Imago Dei*. Multitudes now more than ever are living on the edge of survival and on the edge of forever. Your faithfulness—and your fruitfulness—matter.

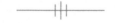

Recommendations

- Read *Prodigal God* by Timothy Keller to review your grasp of the gospel.
- Read Joshua Crossman's The Great Opportunity (you can find it here: www.thegreatopportunity.org) and assess how your own church or organization is living into these realities and recommendations.
- Share this book with ten other leaders in your own ecosystem of relationships, and discuss in what ways you can apply it locally.

Chapter 2

DISRUPTED

In 2020, the world's eyes turned to New York City as it became the global epicenter of the COVID-19 pandemic. Nearly 20,000 people in New York City died from the coronavirus.[1] This was more than twice the number of COVID-19 deaths in all of Germany.[2] It was six times greater than the number of deaths from September 11, 2001.[3] The city experienced so much death that every day during the pandemic, unidentified corpses were taken to Hart Island off of the Bronx.[4]

The devastation this virus produced took on apocalyptic levels. And many people realized the wild unpredictability of life. Fear and anxiety raced through cities and neighborhoods everywhere, as people wondered what would happen to their livelihoods, the future economy, and travel routines. People even began to wonder how much longer they would live. Nothing was certain anymore. COVID-19 became the great disruptor.

Disruption is not new to New York City, which has experienced nearly 250 years of it, dating back to the Great Fire of

1776. Yet something remarkable happened to many churches during this COVID-19 period of disruption. The great disruption created a divine disruption of how people view their own sense of security. People began to turn toward spiritual things, seeking God and the stability of faith during this time. Immediately after the outbreak in March 2020, I surveyed twenty New York City area churches to compare pre-COVID church attendance with post-COVID online attendance. The results were stunning: average church attendance went up more than 100 percent.[5]

While we rejoiced in how God was moving, we can take deeper lessons from what happened. In fact, we can take lessons not only from this experience but from further back. History has much to teach us, especially in terms of what happens in periods of disruption. If we look closely, we see that spiritual awakenings—revivals—are always a sign of God's stirring when a community, city, nation, or even nations are experiencing major disruption. It is important for us to look back at history, because it helps us become conscious of opportunities in the current moment in which God creates a new environment. Amid extraordinary, world-history-altering disruption, God moves in powerful, unprecedented ways. One important lesson we learn is that the scope of a revival is in proportion to the depth of disruption that precedes that awakening.

As in many spiritual awakenings, there is a backstory taking place. For instance, fifty years ago, the Jesus Movement among young people took place during the unrest of the Vietnam War. Let's look at some of the major disruptions New York City has experienced throughout her history and how God responded.

New York City and the American Revolution
(1775-1783)

When America was still a collection of British-ruled colonies, New York City was the epicenter of British control because of the ease of shipping in and out of its harbors. As the Revolutionary War broke out, New York also served as a center of commerce. In 1776, so the story goes, revolutionaries were attempting to disrupt British commerce from taking place in Manhattan and so they torched the city. The devastation that became known as the Great Fire of 1776, took out 493 buildings, including one-third of Manhattan's infrastructure.[6]

While people's eyes were on the devastation and the military revolution, another revolution was taking place—a spiritual revolution. And we see no greater results than what occurred in the African-American community. The spiritual revolution emerging in New York City was the birth of the African-American church on the heels of the American Revolution. Peter Williams, an African American from John Street Methodist Church, founded the first black church in New York City. Williams proposed to his church that they purchase his freedom and he would repay the church. They agreed and he kept his word, repaying them in three years. In 1800, Williams founded the first African Methodist Episcopal Zion church on the corner of Church and Leonard streets.

Sixteen years later, Abyssinian Baptist began in Harlem. Abyssinian grew so large and influential that it became the largest Protestant church in America in the nineteenth century. The disruption of the Great Fire and the American Revolution saw God's hand at work through the emergence of the African-American church in New York City. "The public mission of the black church," Robert Franklin writes, "was to compel America to become America for everyone."[7] It would become the conscience of the nation in the tortuously slow journey toward freedom.

The Fulton Street Revival (1857-1858)

In 1857, 30,000 men stood idle in the streets of New York City because of the financial crash of that year. Drunkenness was rampant. The nation was divided over the issue of slavery. Against this backdrop of financial, moral, and racial malaise, church attendance was declining. In an effort to respond to the decline, New York's Reformed Church denomination hired Jeremiah Lanphier as a lay evangelist to bring people to their services.

After weeks of fruitless labors, in desperation, Lanphier decided to hold a noontime prayer meeting on September 23, 1857, to ask God to stir spiritual interest in the citizens of New York City. He worked overtime to get the word out via flyers to the general population that he was hosting the prayer meeting in the basement of the Fulton Street Church, located near Wall Street in lower Manhattan. That day, Lanphier waited for people to show up. For thirty minutes he waited. Just as he began to give up hope, he heard footsteps coming down the stairs. Eventually six people came and prayed for change. The time together was so empowering for them, they decided to continue meeting weekly and would invite others to join them.

The next week fourteen showed up. Twenty-three came the week after. The fourth week, their number grew to forty. Within a matter of weeks, thousands were praying at noontime in various locations across New York City. They prayed that God would awaken individuals to respond in salvation to His calling. They prayed for the financial well-being of individuals and the city.

God answered. Revival had come! The spiritual awakening that began in Manhattan spread northward to Boston, southward to Philadelphia, and westward to Cleveland. Over the course of the next two years, more than 1 million people converted to Christianity.[8] In New York City churches were seeing 10,000 conversions a week during the season of 1857–1858.[9] This spiritual awakening became known as the Fulton Street Revival.

But that was just the beginning. A financial crisis, as well as the looming Civil War, created the spiritual environment for a longer spiritual awakening, which took place from 1865 to 1920.

Salvation in the Slums (1865–1920)

During the Civil War and for decades after, from 1860 to 1920, New York City experienced a population boom as more and more people from other parts of the country, as well as those from outside the country, moved to NYC seeking jobs and to better their living situation. The city grew from 800,000 in 1860[10] to 5.62 million in 1920, fueled mostly (40 percent) by immigration.[11] Freed African-American slaves also migrated from the rural south to New York City in the hopes of finding work and a better life.

But with the extraordinary growth came extraordinary poverty. This five-decade period in which the country suffered through the Civil War and World War I was a wrenching season for America. New York City felt the effects. And in addition to the major population dislocation, the country, with New York City as one of its leaders, was entering into an industrial era.

Again, a spiritual work was taking place as well. In *Salvation in the Slums*, Norris Magnuson captures the impact of churches, agencies, and leaders during this period. The Evangelical Social Work movement birthing is attributed to William Booth, founder of the Salvation Army. Working in East London, Booth preached a gospel of salvation even as his army cared for the desperately poor. As Magnuson points out, Booth's vision and organization also took root in New York City. It has been an enduring movement active in 131 countries today,[12] but New York City felt the impact as its churches and Christian agencies led the way to serving and reaching the city's most impoverished.

Two of the movements that characterized the spirit of this awakening were the Christian and Missionary Alliance (CM&A) and The Bowery Mission. The CM&A was led by A. B. Simpson, its founder in 1890. Simpson became a towering figure in the history of New York City's Christendom with his commitment to the poor and to foreign missions.

The CM&A programs included a rescue home for women; a training college for missionaries, evangelists, and rescue workers; an orphanage; and several rescue missions. Part of Simpson's legacy is also Nyack College and Seminary, which is located on 2 Washington Street in downtown Manhattan and is still a vital part of the city and ministry.[13] The first converts of the alliance were among the poor, and Simpson asserted that "the great majority of our people are actively engaged either in rescue work at home or evangelistic work abroad."[14] Simpson adopted the model of a monthly all-night prayer meeting for their slum workers. Again, God responded, and by 1895, the CM&A was not only seeing the poor give their lives to Christ, but the church had also sent out nearly 300 missionaries into global missions.[15]

Many people came to Manhattan looking for work but had no place to live. Homeless missions emerged as a compassionate response to the many homeless in Manhattan. And The Bowery Mission answered the call. The Bowery Mission, the third oldest homeless mission in America, was an arm of the *Christian Herald*. More than any other publication, the *Christian Herald* drew national attention to the plight of the homeless. Its readership grew to 250,000 people, making it one of the most broadly read publications in the world.[16]

The Bowery Mission was the *Christian Herald*'s way to put feet to the message. By 1890 it was housing 150 men and providing 7,000 meals per day.[17] Today The Bowery Mission provides 400,000 meals a year.

At a national level, the needs of freed slaves were enormous. African Americans were expected to navigate a newfound freedom without basic educational skills and economic opportunities. During the post-Civil War trauma of reconstruction, another spiritual movement was underfoot. Baptist and Methodist missionaries were teaching freed slaves to read. Leaders were being educated, and newly literate African Americans began to grow existing African-American churches, such as the African Methodist Episcopal Church and the African Methodist Zion churches, and birthing others. There became an extraordinary movement of planting churches, which led to a large-scale number of conversions. In less than thirty years after the Civil War, more than 2.7 million out of 8.5 million former slaves were Christian.[18]

In *Beyond Liberation*, Carl Ellis notes that between 1865 and 1900, more African Americans became Christian than any other ethnic group in American history.[19] This was directly attributable to the work of Baptist and Methodist missionaries—as a response of God's hand working through disruption. African-American churches are such at the heart of God's spiritual work through disruption that we cannot understand the gospel in cities apart from the vibrancy and strength of the African-American church in cities. The epicenter of the church in New York City is the African-American church in Brooklyn, due to the sheer number and strength of her churches.

Ellis Island (1891–1954)

When looking at New York City's population boom, we would be remiss not to consider immigration. Ellis Island was opened as a port of entry for immigrants in 1891. Between 1892 and 1954, 12 million immigrants passed through Ellis Island.[20] This immigration was marked by a strong Jewish and Catholic population from southern and eastern Europe. It also caused New

York City to pivot from being a primarily Protestant city to a significant Jewish and Catholic center. Modern-day New York City is the second largest Jewish city in the world, after Tel Aviv, with more than 1 million Jewish people living in New York City today.[21]

The city was disrupted by the enormous influx of immigrants. The religious landscape was changing radically and quickly. As Catholic immigrants came pouring into New York from Ireland, the Protestant community would not allow access to schools and hospitals. As a result, the Catholic church built its own institutions. One of the great legacies of the Catholic church is its enduring schools and hospitals giving the city some of its great institutions.

The strength of the Catholic church is captured in a photograph in *American Catholic,* which shows 100,000 Irish Catholics lining Fifth Avenue in Manhattan to celebrate the building of Saint Patrick's Cathedral. This cathedral was an extraordinary achievement given the plight of Irish immigrants. Nearly 10 percent of Irish citizens starved to death during the potato famine of the 1840s. Immigrants came to the shores of New York starving, disorganized, and looking for hope. They found it in New York City. Within thirty years a new immigrant community built a cathedral.

Since their arrival in New York City, the Catholic community has built many of our finest schools and hospitals and has significantly enriched our institutional strength as a city. The Catholic church has also provided many of the most significant charitable organizations. Today Catholic Charities is a federation of more than ninety agencies serving the needs of the poor in New York City.

The economic crash of 1929 ushered in the Great Depression.

God in the Garden (1957)

Billy Graham was preaching in New York during that period between the end of World War II and the civil rights movement of the 1950s and 1960s. There was a lot simmering underneath the surface regarding the inequities of race and the flight of white evangelicals out of the city fueled by inexpensive housing. Graham's message was that only the gospel could address the greatest needs of the human heart in being reconciled to God and to each other.

Evangelist Billy Graham had a unique relationship with New York City. In 1957, Graham preached in Madison Square Garden for 100 consecutive nights. Over the course of that year's summer, 56,000 people made decisions for Christ. During that same 100-day period Graham preached to 100,000 people at Yankee Stadium with 20,000 people being turned away. This is the largest gathering in the history of Yankee Stadium, the citadel of baseball.[22] The summer crusade ended on September 1 at an outdoor rally in Times Square with 125,000 people jamming Broadway.

On September 22, 1991, Graham returned to New York City to preach in Central Park. The day before the event, I remember Dr. Graham coming to Times Square Church where we held a concert of prayer for the gathering that next day.[23] God responded. Graham preached to 250,000 people, the largest religious gathering in his career.

Graham again returned for his final crusade career and preached June 24–26, 2005, in Flushing Meadow Park. The Sunday before the crusade, Graham attended a reception where I had the opportunity to sit with him. He was eighty-six years old and frail. Remarkably, when he got up to preach on June 24, just as the sun was setting, he had extraordinary energy. It was a poignant final New York City engagement. It was God's hand once again responding to disruption with fruitfulness.

The Immigration Act (1966)

Amid the civil rights movement came a growing consciousness of racial diversity in our nation. New York City had hosted the World's Fair in 1939 and 1964 in Flushing Meadow Park in Queens. Eager for a better way of life, the nations came to our city to see New York.

To respond to the growing desire for people to come to this country, President Lyndon B. Johnson signed the Immigration Act in 1966. This legislation opened wide the doors for immigrants to enter the country. Immigrants by the hundreds of thousands from Asia, Africa, and Latin America poured into New York City. As the immigrants came, they brought with them the fruit of the revivals that were spreading across Korea, China, Africa, the Caribbean, and South America.

As we look at today's landscape of active Christians in New York City, I estimate that more than 90 percent are either immigrant or minority.[24] By 1990, First Baptist Church of Flushing had attendees from sixty language groups and forty denominational backgrounds. Our Flushing neighborhood spoke more than 100 languages. Today, New York City speaks more than 800 languages.

One of the great phenomena in New York City is the Pentecostal churches birthed from immigrants from Puerto Rico and the Dominican Republic. It seems that the Azusa Street Revival that introduced Pentecostalism into the United States on April 9, 1906, spread rapidly to the Caribbean, and boomeranged back to New York City.

Three Decades of Trauma (1970–2000)

In the 1970s, New York was teetering on the verge of bankruptcy. In his famous message to the city, President Gerald Ford denied a financial bailout. As a conservative politician, Ford had an antagonistic relationship with the liberal city. The *New York Post* famously gave the headline, "Ford to City: Drop Dead."[25] Not only was the city broke, the Bronx was burning. An estimated 97 percent of seven census tracts in the Bronx burned to the ground or were abandoned as landlords torched properties for insurance money rather than attempt to rent vacant buildings.[26]

More disruption hit New York City as the crack cocaine epidemic arrived in the 1980s. Between 1982 and 1985, there were 1.6 million users in the United States, and NYC was not immune. The drug was especially vicious in the African-American communities like Harlem, where the lure of making money from drug trafficking decimated neighborhoods. The criminalization of low-level offenders resulted in a significant spike in the prison population.[27]

The drug epidemic also fueled a murder epidemic that began in earnest in December 1984 when Bernard Goetz, a German American, shot four unarmed African Americans on the subway. The murder rate escalated for a decade, culminating in 1993 with eight murders a day for a year. So many people died that the city morgue ran out of room.[28]

Against this backdrop, from 1984 to 1994, churches were feeling powerless to cope with the enormity of crime and despair in the city. I was on staff with InterVarsity Christian Fellowship. During my tenure there, in 1987, I heard of a citywide prayer gathering in Chicago at Moody Church and thought that our city needed something similar. I approached Ted Gandy and Aida Force of Here's Life about holding a New York City gathering. Here's Life began in New York City in 1976 with the "I Found It" campaign to reach multitudes with the gospel. They agreed with my proposition.

The following year, on February 5, 1988, we invited sixteen churches to participate in our first concert of prayer gathering, which David Bryant, founder of Concerts of Prayer International, would lead, and which we hosted at First Baptist Church of Flushing, Queens, my home church. That night sixteen churches didn't attend; seventy-five churches attended. The response spoke to the hunger of Christians in New York

City to unite and to ask God to perform miraculously in our city.

That first prayer gathering was not only the opportunity for churches to come together and pray for our city's awakening, it was also an opportunity for churches to experience fellowship with one another and to share one another's burdens. It was so successful, we decided to do it again seven months later. Over the next thirty years, Concerts of Prayer continued yearly gatherings and saw 2,000 churches and 250,000 people participate in diverse prayer gatherings. We also saw God's hand at work in two macro answers to prayer: (1) from 1994 to 2014, the murder rate declined by 90 percent; (2) from 1989 to 2014, evangelical Christianity grew in Manhattan by 500 percent.

Churches praying together in the 1980s and 1990s prepared us for the terrorist attacks and trauma of September 11, 2001. Our Concerts of Prayer Greater New York board was sitting on the fifteenth floor of the Empire State Building when the first tower was struck. Thirty minutes later, the second tower was hit. We scrambled down to Fifth Avenue where we saw smoke from the explosion two miles south billowing across the avenue.

After banding together for a decade in prayer for NYC, in the ensuing weeks following 9/11, we knew and trusted one another well enough that we committed to work together to alleviate the pain of the city. Churches across all five boroughs and beyond mobilized to feed the unemployed, and hundreds of volunteers provided pastoral counseling at Ground Zero. Our Concerts of Prayer team worked with World Vision to raise $6 million to assist victims of 9/11 through local churches.

In retrospect, I wonder if the days of 9/11 were part of God's providential plan as a warmup for the necessary scale of COVID-19 relief. In the aftermath of 9/11 and the 2008 financial crisis, God has providentially used these disruptions to cause us to see the world differently and more tenderly. We saw the brokenness and fragility of the world—and in particular, our city—in technicolor.

The Lesson in All of This

In chapter 1 we looked at the concept that the speed of the gospel in a city is in proportion to the depth of unity between members of the same ecosystem. When we apply that to New York City and review 250 years of its history, we see that the greatness of a coming spiritual awakening is in proportion to the depth of disruption that precedes the awakening. Disruption comes to us and to our cities politically, financially, physically, and socially. Whether it be the Great Fire of 1776 or the Great Crash of 2008, God is inviting us to lean into the moment as a community of Jesus followers to demonstrate the ancient truth of Augustine—that the City of God is both invisible and imperishable.

That truth invites us to be radically committed to one another and to the needs of those around us. Nothing like COVID-19 has happened in 100 years. Is it possible that God can use our intentional, tenacious unity to cause more fruit to be born in New York City than at any other point in our history?

The Brooklyn Bridge against the backdrop of Downtown Manhattan

Chapter 3

THE GREAT OPPORTUNITY

On January 16, 2020, Josh Crossman, author of *The Great Opportunity*, and CEO and director of the Pinetops Foundation, addressed US Movement Day city leaders in Los Angeles. In his remarks, Crossman said, "Of all the young people we interviewed, the only ones who could articulate their beliefs were the children of Mormon parents."[1]

Why do Mormon children have a higher retention in their faith? According to Crossman, because of three reasons:

- Highly engaged parents who care for their own faith
- Other supporting adults
- Calling youth into mission[2]

This is an indictment against many of our churches and families who have failed to disciple their children effectively. In *The Great Opportunity*, Crossman writes, "The base case scenario represents a profound shift: over 1 million young people every year—children who were in our Sunday schools, youth groups, confirmation classes, our mission trips—are saying that

Christ is no longer He with whom they choose to identify. . . .
They left because they just weren't interested in the Christian
life they saw."[3]

The result of this dramatic shift is the forecasted loss of forty-two million young people from the American church by the
year 2050. Unless something changes, a secondary consequence
of this shift will be the closure of 50 percent of all churches in
America. As Crossman writes, "The majority of religious switch-
ing takes place by 25 and religious preference remains constant
after age 35."[4] When we extrapolate the impact on our country and
the globe with the disappearance of tens of thousands of American churches in a COVID reality, it is genuinely frightening.

In a conference call with Khary Bridgewater from the
DeVoss Foundation, Bridgewater said, "We have lost twenty
bishops within the Church of God in Christ denomination in
two months. African-American churches, which represent the
frontlines in addressing the needs of the inner city, are being
decimated after the virus."[5]

But amid this terrifying scenario, Crossman writes about
the positive possibilities—the great opportunity:

> We are at a pivotal moment in the life of the American
> church. [We are facing] the largest missions opportunity
> ever in American history. . . . If we return to retention
> and evangelism like we saw just 20 years ago, more peo-
> ple will be saved than during both Great Awakenings,
> the African American church growth after the Civil
> War, the Azusa revival, and every Billy Graham conver-
> sion combined. . . . It is worth noting that all Christians
> in America still comprise the majority (59 percent) of
> the religious affiliation in our base case."[6]

As we have seen the great disruption of New York City and how God responded over and over with historic spiritual revivals, I am convinced He is moving again. This is our great opportunity, as Crossman asserts. And the most strategic place to start in creating momentum toward the re-evangelization of the United States is in New York City.

What We Can Do About It

As we seek to reverse the current trend and guide ourselves toward the greatest mission's opportunity in American history, we are not without vision. Crossman provides us with five sound strategies. We need only read his work to realize that what is already happening in New York City is a validation of his insight. Just as it was in the New Testament, where the gospel spread through the great cities of the first century, what happens in New York City will influence the globe. And we have the "great opportunity" to be part of seeing it happen as we turn our eyes toward our 2030 plan for Metro New York City.

Let's look briefly at each of Crossman's strategies, and then in the following chapters, we'll unpack them more to see how we can actually use and build on those strategies to create a new and exciting church reality.

Strategy #1: Start New Churches

Four thousand churches are started each year. That is the good news. The bad news is that each year 3,700 churches will close. Added to that reality is that many pastors are aging and retiring. For us to see the kind of renewal that will change the trajectory, we need to get aggressive in our church-planting efforts and start 8,000 churches annually in the United States.[7]

Crossman believes that a priority for new church plants

needs to be urban, minority, and in the Northeast. The Northeast has 18 percent of the United States population and 11 percent of all churches in the United States.[8] As a northeastern city with a high minority population, New York City is a high priority in the church-planting world.

As we discussed briefly in chapter 1, churches ten years and younger are six to eight times more effective in reaching new people than churches older than ten years. Fueling the 300 percent growth of the evangelical church in Manhattan from 1989 to 2009 was that, from 2001 to 2009, church leaders planted 39 percent of all churches in Manhattan. Manhattan church planting has been a strength to the city gospel movement in New York City over the past thirty years, thanks to the work of City to City and several denominational networks. This dramatic church growth in Manhattan is an incredibly significant sign of hope to the globe.

The current United States population is 331 million people. The Metro NYC population is 19 million, or approximately 6 percent of the nation.[9] In our collective work, we have seen a 500 percent growth in the evangelical church in Manhattan from 1989 to 2014. Looking ahead, if we see even a 5 percent response to the gospel in Metro NYC within the next decade, it would result in nearly 1 million conversions. Even conservatively speaking, based on our current knowledge of church planting, that number could be 100,000 new people joining our churches.

Strategy #2: Create Significant Mission Opportunities for Youth

I have experienced and observed in my own spiritual journey the necessity of engaging children, high-school-age, and college-age young people. I came to faith at age seventeen, and at the age of twenty-one, at the Urbana '79 missions conference, I knew I was called to a lifetime commitment to missions work, along with my wife, Marya. We dedicated our lives to it at that conference. I had been given a significant mission opportunity and I was ready and willing to accept. Working with university students for the next thirteen years, I witnessed how many major life decisions are made by the age of twenty-two.

Just as I felt part of something bigger and more meaningful when I stepped into missions, today's young people are aching for that same sense of significance. As Crossman suggests in his second strategy, "The practical cause of disaffiliation is that their understanding of the person of Jesus from their childhood and teen years was not sufficient to keep them in relationship with Him into adulthood."[10]

To change that, he suggests giving our youth a sense of mission. We do that when we:

- Equip and mobilize the whole church to foster youth formation
- Provide parents tools for teaching their children
- Equip and send youth into missions opportunities
- Build a national advocacy model for youth formation[11]

Metro New York City has some of the most robust youth outreach efforts in America. We have world-class leaders and organizations like Young Life, Youth for Christ, InterVarsity, Cru, The Navigators, and Thrive Collective. As an InterVarsity staff member in New York City for thirteen years, I have seen the transformative impact investing strategically in young adults can have.

As the result of my own missions commitment at Urbana '79, in 1983, at the age of twenty-four, I, along with my wife, Marya, committed to go to North India. We were plunged into Bihar, India, a state that has 100 million people—and a ratio of 100,000 to 1, Hindus and Muslims to Christians. That summer we were involved in open-air evangelism, campus-evangelistic Bible studies, home groups, and discipleship training with our team of young Indian men. We experienced the full spectrum of being overwhelmed by a massive population density, living in a hostile religious environment, and experiencing the extraordinary courage of followers of Jesus. This body of experiences prepared Marya and me to sell our possessions and move to New York City a year later.

I have seen this same pattern in the next generation. In 2002, with that same vision to empower my seventeen-year-old daughter, Anna, into the significance of mission, I took her with me to East Africa. We traveled to see the impact of the HIV/AIDS pandemic killing 3 million people a year. We were there specifically to mobilize churches to engage the realities of widows and orphans through World Vision. Over the course of a decade, churches in Metro NYC and Pennsylvania sponsored 11,000 children, impacting 600,000 people. Even New York City's influence touches small villages on the other side of the world.

While we were there, I watched the transformation that took place in my daughter as she developed a passion for the orphan and the widow. And that significant sense of mission stayed with her: three years later, she returned to Africa to spend a summer working in a Ugandan orphanage. She also worked in our office assisting churches to sponsor thousands of children through World Vision. During our time in Africa in 2002, I was reading the biography of Mother Teresa who received her call at age seventeen. God powerfully uses seventeen-year-olds.

Imagine if we strategically invested in our young people. Collectively we believe that we will impact 250,000 young people in the next decade through the aggregate efforts of churches and agencies working together. They are ready for the call—and the church working collectively can provide it.

Strategy #3: Pursue New Audiences

Though many churches were more in the early stages of using technology—some engaged creatively, while others avoiding it at all costs—the COVID environment forced churches to use technological platforms to reach their own congregants as well as new people.

As churches consider new ways to use technology, Crossman offers some recommendations:

- Create a strong outward-facing brand targeted at the unaffiliated
- Invest in a studio that produces high-quality multimedia content to reach the unaffiliated through social networks
- Provide social-media resources for thoughtful Christians, pastors, and public voices
- Improve the online presence of local churches in their neighborhoods[12]

In May 2020, as mentioned in chapter 1, I invited twenty Metro NYC churches to take a survey on their attendance pre-COVID and for the first four weeks after the shelter-in orders. The churches were ethnically, denominationally, and geographically diverse. Overall, the average attendance per church grew by more than 100 percent.

Metro NYC Church Survey – 19 Churches	Attendance	
Pre Covid	11.904	
Post Covid (4 weeks)	25,921	
Increase	13, 983	118%

Carey Nieuwhof, a prominent Christian thought leader, former attorney, and founding pastor of Connexus Church, wrote in his April 2020 blog:

> **49% of all churches are growing right now.**
>
> A month earlier, before the pandemic hit the West, the statistic would have been that between 8-15% of all churches were growing.
>
> So literally in thirty days, we've moved from a tiny percentage of churches growing to virtually half of all churches growing.
>
> What's even more surprising is that the growth trend holds up in every church size category.
>
> According to the weekly polling we're doing through Church Pulse Weekly (my new podcast/project with Barna and Gloo . . .), half of all churches, regardless of church size—from very small churches (under 100) to megachurches—are experiencing growth. It's remarkable that this is true if you have 75 people attending, 750 or 7500.[13]

The new COVID realities make Crossman's recommendations more urgent in this new season. The future of the church in America will be largely influenced by the speed of our pivot into the digital age.

Strategy #4: Care for the Poor

On May 8, 2020, the United States April job loss was reported at 20,500,000. It is the steepest job loss since the Great Depression.[14] In New York City, job losses translate to creating more pressure on emergency food services. One food pantry, Reaching

Out Community Services in Brooklyn, has had to wrestle with closing down given the virus. Their founder, Thomas Neve, said that if they closed, they could not assist the 10,000 people who rely on them for food security.[15]

The *New York Times* reported on May 6, 2020, that the "food bank for New York City usually supplies about 1,000 institutions, such as food pantries and soup kitchens, with groceries. Now, 40 percent of them have suspended operations because of the coronavirus outbreak, said Leslie Gordon, chief executive of Food Bank for New York City."[16]

Pre-COVID, an estimated 1.4 million New York City residents relied on emergency food programs, including soup kitchens and food pantries, each year. Approximately 339,000 New York City children, or approximately one out of every five rely on soup kitchens and food pantries.[17] The new reality paints a grim picture. It also opens an enormous door of opportunity.

The opportunity in front of us is to appropriately draw attention to the good works of the church in caring for the poor. New York City has had some of the most extraordinary agencies caring for the impoverished in American history. Given the intensification of poverty dynamics during COVID-19, this is an unprecedented opportunity to impact the poor not just in the immediate but in the long term. We believe conservatively that we will impact 250,000 people collectively through our aggregate efforts in the next decade.

Strategy #5: Build Long-Term Witness for Generations to Come

The university is the most strategic portal into culture. It is where future leaders, homemakers, and thought leaders are shaped. Yet according to Crossman, only 2 to 5 percent of the faculty in the top forty universities are Christian.[18] Crossman quotes Princeton professor J. Gresham Machen who said, "We may preach with all the fervor of a reformer and yet succeed only in winning a straggler here and there, if we permit the whole collective thought of the nation or of the world to be controlled by ideas which, by the resistless force of logic, prevent Christianity from being regarded as anything more than a harmless delusion."[19]

This is an exciting yet daunting reality in Metro New York City with more than ninety universities and 600,000 university students. It is arguably the most strategic mission field in the world in the most influential city in the world. Dozens of chapters of InterVarsity, Cru, and The Navigators are sprinkled across these campuses. One of the greatest needs in our region is to create a more effective pipeline from the local church youth group to the university chapters of active Christians.

To do that, Crossman recommends for us to:

- Invest earlier in leadership development by vision casting and formation for high-potential Christian undergraduates
- Encourage more Christian scholars to enter the academy as a calling equal to ministry or professional vocations
- Launch a regular convening to gather cross-disciplinary groups of Christians
- Increase long-horizon philanthropic investments in leadership development[20]

These strategies call for us to embrace the gospel ecosystem to meaningfully accelerate these efforts city by city. We need the awareness, aggregation, and coordination of effort to be effective. We cannot think that attempting these strategies with the spirit of American individualism on our own will effect meaningful change. We are all in this together. But think of what that means.

Imagine what 2030 will look like as the result of thousands of new churches being planted, tens of thousands of young people committing to a lifetime of fruitful mission, the poor rejoicing in the generosity and inclusion they receive from churches, and marketplace leaders being unleashed to their full potential to impact this great city. Each of us has a part to play in shaping God's preferred future for our cities.

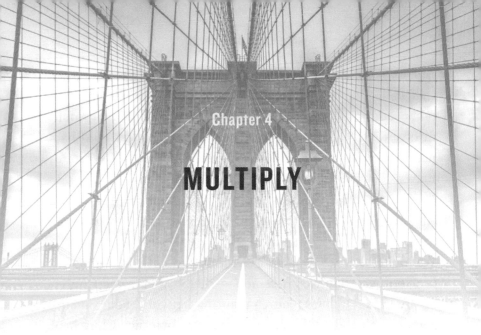

Chapter 4

MULTIPLY

I was standing in my kitchen in June 1987 when the phone rang. Marya and I were living in Flushing, Queens, at the time. The voice on the other end of the phone was Tim Keller's. I had no idea who Keller was. He introduced himself and said he was coming to New York City to do research for an eventual church plant. Keller had been teaching at Westminster Seminary in Philadelphia, but when the leaders in the Presbyterian Church of America denomination approached him to get into planting and pastoral work, he agreed to take the plunge and plant a church in Manhattan.

Two years later, in 1989, Redeemer Presbyterian Church officially began in Manhattan with a vision to multiply churches. For the past two decades, Redeemer and its agency Redeemer City to City have planted 400 churches in cities globally.

A decade later Keller called me again. This time he wanted to talk about creating a church-planting alliance. He invited me to a breakfast at Sbarro's restaurant in Manhattan in 2000 along with two of his colleagues, Dick Kauffman from the Redeemer staff and Glen Kleinknecht from Here's Life Inner City. He proposed that we create a church-planting alliance that would involve diverse denominations and networks and would harness Redeemer's church-planting expertise with Concerts of Prayer's convening ability. We decided to pursue it.

In 2003, we officially birthed the Church Multiplying Alliance (CMA), after multiple conversations with denominational leaders and initial fundraising to support the effort. We invited numerous denominations and networks—including Southern Baptists, Assemblies of God, Reformed Church of America, Orchard Church planting network, Four Square, Missouri Synod Lutheran, and the Presbyterian Church of America—to get involved with our vision. They agreed, and with everyone on board and ready to get to work, the CMA began hosting semi-annual vision-casting meetings, which led to identifying church planters. Redeemer then began to train those leaders.

In the 1980s, Manhattan church attendance had been 1 percent. If the CMA followed Keller's vision to see 10 percent of Manhattan residents attending Bible-believing churches, we knew that would represent a growth of 135,000 people attending church. We had a lot of work to do. But we also knew new churches were essential to God's strategy to impact Manhattan.

God indeed blessed the work, and by 2009, our research indicated that within a decade, attendance in New York City evangelical churches represented a 300-percent growth—going from 1 percent to 3 percent church attendance (see graph in chapter 1). This research motivated the birth of Movement Day. The research was so stunning that we knew others would want to know about it and learn from each of our respective city movements.

Five years later, in 2014, City to City commissioned research to help us gauge how our efforts were fairing. The research indicated that the percentage of people now attending Bible-believing churches in Manhattan was at 5 percent.[1] That fueled everyone's passion to the commitment. In 2016, City to City began a campaign to plant 1,000 evangelical churches of all types in New York City by 2026, which would include traditional building-based churches, house churches, and bivo-cational pastor-led churches.

Though 1,000 churches seem like a lot in a decade, let's not forget that Josh Crossman believes we need *8,000* new churches annually to address the attrition of older churches and to reach new populations.

As we learned in chapter 3, we have strategies to put in place to keep the church, particularly in New York City, alive and vibrant. Starting in this chapter and continuing through chapter 7, we will look more closely and practically at each of those strategies. In this chapter, let us turn our attention toward the first of those strategies: planting and multiplying churches.

A Ten-Year Vision for Multiplication

On May 5, 2020, I interviewed Robert Guerrero and Jon Tyson to capture their thoughts and insight regarding church planting in New York City. Guerrero is a Redeemer City to City Vice President Catalyst for Church Planting, and Tyson is the senior pastor of Church for the City in Manhattan. Rather than try to summarize their words, I present our conversation below:[2]

MAC PIER: How would you describe the recent history of church planting?

ROBERT GUERRERO: We are seeing an acceleration of effort. In the decade from 2006 to 2016, we saw 100 new churches planted through our network of church plants. In the past four years, from 2016 to 2020, we have seen fifty-one new churches. Twenty of those churches are city-center Manhattan and thirty-one new churches are in the boroughs. Currently, we are training ninety Millennial leaders in six incubator programs. We see a day when we can train more than 100 church planters every year.

JON TYSON: Our church helped plant eleven congregations in the Trinity Grace Network between 2005 and 2017. These eleven churches would have received benefit from City to City training and funding.

RG: The Trinity Grace Network created a pivotal moment in the church-planting movement. Their footprint was all over Manhattan. The TGN saw itself as a family in a parish model. Churches were adopting their neighborhoods. TGN congregations were diverse churches, which reflected the cosmopolitan nature of the city by their diversity.

MPP: COVID-19 has been a game-changer for the way we "do" church and attract nonbelievers. What have you seen in this COVID environment?

RG: There is more openness beyond the traditional-launch model of starting churches (starting in a building with a core group). COVID is pushing all churches to rethink their methods. C3 church planting, for example, has been using dinner parties to plant new churches, which obviously limits the number of people who attend. Now their gatherings have become virtual. They have attracted up to 2,000 in online attendance.

MPP: In 2012, in Astoria, Queens, Drew Hyun created a network called Hope Churches, which currently has ten Hope churches with an aggregate attendance of between 2,000 and 2,500. He and Edwin Colon of Recovery House of Worship have also created the New City Network, which has assisted twenty-five church plants globally. In 2016, their network began hosting an annual conference. That first year they had 175 attendees and have been growing ever since, the most recent one selling out at 350 attendees.[3] What other stories of innovation have you heard?

RG: We are seeing some exciting models involving community engagement and bi-vocational leadership. The Latino Pastoral Action Center, which Raymond Rivera leads, has been engaging their community with a charter school and offering programming to assist the underprivileged. A Southern Baptist immigrant bi-vocational church planter, Plinio Vaez, has a congregation that meets in the basement of a laundromat. They have been so effective that they are now sending out missionaries into the city.

MPP: What does it take to become an effective church planter in New York City?

JT: Churches need to be networked together. We are an ecosystem of relationships. I am indebted to leaders like

Adam Durso from LEAD.NYC [see chapter 6] and Walter Sotelo from CitiVision, who have networked me into the larger body of Christ throughout the city.

RG: Church planters need to be rooted to their communities. For those leaders who come to New York City from outside, we challenge them to get a job and get the city under their fingernails. We describe this as the "Galilean Journey," where Jesus had to be a carpenter for thirty years before He began His public ministry. Only then do we feel leaders are prepared to join our incubator program to get the training they need to launch a church.

MPP: Part of our mission is to look ahead to the next decade to see what is possible as we grow the body of Christ. What is your vision for 2030?

JT: I would like to see the majority of people coming to churches from unchurched backgrounds. We want to see more baptisms with a deeper, embedded discipleship within churches. We want to see life-on-life discipleship.

RG: We have a current project, which City to City oversees, to plant 270 New York City churches by 2026. In the broader scope of church planting, we envision 1,000 church plants with the various networks contributing their efforts (including such groups as Southern Baptists, Assemblies of God, Hillsong, Orchard, Hope Network). The average church grows to seventy people, given our space constraints and need for nontraditional forms of church planting. Our incubator program can potentially train more than 1,000 leaders by 2030 to plant churches of all types.

MPP: To get us from where we are to where we need to be by 2030, what must happen?

JT: We need to see God bring revival and spiritual awakening through aggressive, united prayer. We in the West are too far gone unless God supernaturally intervenes.

RG: Given the demographics of New York City churches, which are more than 90 percent minority, we need to highlight the work of minority church planters. Minority leaders need to see themselves as part of the strategy to impact the city.

Getting to the Fruitfulness God Desires

The gospel reminds us that Jesus lived the life we should live, and He died the death we deserve. In His death, Jesus put death to death. What drove Jesus to His death was His not wanting anyone to be on the outside of His redemptive work. With great honor, He invites us to enter into His passion for others by planting churches that bear great fruit. This is how we can get started.

Recommendation #1: Make Prayer the Central Priority

God wants His people to pray—not just individually but corporately. We must be united in our prayer efforts (more on this in chapter 9). The work of spiritual conversion ultimately rests with God and the mystery of how He works. In 1989, 500 congregations, an estimated 100,000 people, prayed daily for Redeemer Presbyterian's successful planting.[4]

Make praying for new church plants a central priority in your personal and congregational life. Jesus Himself told us to pray that God would raise us workers in the harvest (Matthew 9:37-38). Look up pray.nyc to join a 24/7 prayer chain. In chapter 8 we will discuss ways to keep this priority in front of every involved church in Metro New York City.

Recommendation #2: Attend Strategic Conferences

Engage the vision to plant churches by attending strategic conferences like *Exponential.* Vision-casting leaders to plant churches is a crucial action step. This happens in several settings through church-planting conferences locally and nationally. This also happens in regular denominational and network settings. In New York City we encourage every interested leader to attend the New City Conference, as we mentioned earlier in the chapter.

Recommendation #3: Participate in a Church-Planting Incubator Program

Any serious church planter in the Metro NYC area should research participation in an incubator program as a next step in learning how to plant churches. Redeemer City to City has extraordinary expertise in training leaders to plant churches through their incubator program. An incubator program is simply a two-year training arrangement that provides a church planter with the expertise to be effective in planting a church. The incubator includes training in four specific arenas: personal/interpersonal skills; communication skills to learn how best to convey both grace and truth; missional culture; and executing visionary leadership. To unite our efforts, every leader and network in Metro NYC can connect viable church-planting candidates to this program.[5]

Recommendation #4: Partner with Church Planters in Metro New York City

It accelerates the gospel ecosystem if we can empower church planters in our community, borough, or region by partnering with other church planters. The work of church planting is long and difficult. And many times, it can bring frustration and hardship. This is when we need others to come alongside for help, encouragement, and inspiration. Church planters need community too. They need to hear about how others are responding to the work and share ideas on what has worked and not worked in engagement efforts with neighbors. We can also consider financial investment to assist a new church plant. We can visit services and consider joint outreaches to scale our impact in a community. To reach our collective goal of 1,000-plus church plants in Metro New York City within the next decade, we will need a high degree of intentionality. To help motivate us in that partnership work, in this chapter's remaining pages, I have included six examples of church plants in Metro New York City. May their work inspire and challenge you in yours.

RENEWAL IN THE WESTERN CHURCH
Jon Tyson Leads Church of the City

Jon Tyson has helped plant eleven churches in Manhattan and the outer boroughs since 2005. As a gifted, perceptive leader, Tyson also created the Trinity Grace Network, which became a vibrant community of churches. When speaking about the status of the modern church in New York City, he gives this analysis: "Manhattan can be described as a place of meaninglessness, despair, and hedonism. It mirrors the broader culture. Unless God brings revival, we will be too far gone. Much of the church of Manhattan is prayerless. I am committed to engage in and model prayer for the city."

Tyson sees a link between aggressive, passionate prayer and fruitful evangelism. Church of the City now has groups that pray four times a day five times a week for an hour each time and engage in five hours of corporate prayer on Sundays. Before the COVID pandemic, the church saw an average of 200 people weekly involved in corporate prayer and meeting in their Manhattan West Side offices. Post-COVID, the prayer meetings have grown in attendance.

They have seen the fruit of their prayers. One example is through the Alpha courses they offer. Alpha is a movement of home-based and small-group apologetics that answers questions seekers have about Christianity. "We had a young woman who came to our church to clean up her act," Tyson says. "It so changed her that she invited forty of her friends to Alpha. She now helps run Alpha for our church." He tells of another young woman who started a small group, which has now multiplied to 150 people. "We empowered these two young women, Rachael and Abby, and they have had an extraordinary impact."

Tyson has researched and intently studied the nature of historic revivals, making him one of the world's main influencers on the subject. "The clock determines the play in any athletic game," he says. "Given the decline of Western culture, our play needs to be that we cry out to God for spiritual awakening."[6]

To better encourage others in the play, Tyson created pray. nyc as a simple online platform. Its stated vision is that "Pray. nyc is a movement of prayer and worship for New York City, which calls the city to seek God, love him passionately, and contend for spiritual awakening in our time." On this platform people can sign up to become part of a 24/7 prayer expression in and for New York City.[7]

Tyson carries the mantle of Jeremiah Lanphier (see chapter 2) in calling the city to prayer. He recognizes that Manhattan is a strategic place to seek not just the renewal of New York, but the renewal of the church globally.

———||| ———

A TREE GROWS IN BROOKLYN
James Roberson and Rasool Berry
Plant Bridge Church in Park Slope

One example of how the ecosystem works is seeing students shaped by university ministry becoming church planters. The training received in the university setting is invaluable to church planters, including learning how to share the gospel in a challenging context.

In Rasool Berry's freshman year at the University of Pennsylvania, God got his attention. He decided to give God what he called "a thirty-day trial." He had lots of questions and found answers through Cru, where he then became involved in his campus fellowship. "It was important to me to integrate the intellectual side of my worldview in order to have an intelligent faith," Berry says.

Berry met James Roberson while they were involved with Cru at their respective colleges. They reconnected several years later when in 2014 Roberson decided to start a church in Park Slope, Brooklyn, and reached out to Berry.

They are committed to being a multiethnic church. "Our church is 85 percent single, 50 to 60 percent black and brown, and 40 percent white and Asian. Our average age is twenty-six," Berry says.

They recognize planting a church—in particular, a multi-ethnic one—is a huge undertaking. They have learned how to shape the lives of the next generation by watching the work of such spiritual giants in the faith as A. R. Bernard, Ray Rivera, and Rick Del Rio. These men have modeled dynamic leadership to a generation of New York City's black, Latino, and other ethnic minority faith leaders. These leaders are also part of Nicky Cruz's creative and courageous legacy. For instance, Cruz, whose dramatic conversion was chronicled in David Wilkerson's *The Cross and the Switchblade,* led A. R. Bernard to faith at the Baptist Temple. The sense of the generations' interconnectedness is important to leaders like Roberson and Berry, and they have learned and incorporated a lot as they planted.

So much so that in just six years, the church now averages 300 in attendance. "We emphasize small groups and the arts," Berry explains. "We tend to attract creatives." Probably because Roberson majored in communications and has a sensibility for art. "We have a heavy investment in worship, including two people from Broadway who help us lead," Roberson says. They address issues of justice, such as mass incarceration. They also host outreach events, such as Soul Café, and combine them with music, dance, and poetry.

Through their efforts, they have seen God at work. "A few years ago," Roberson says, "I was asked to speak at Flatbush Reformed Church for pulpit supply. That day a woman named Mindy, who was trying to find herself, saw the church and wanted to see the architecture as an artist. The sanctuary could seat 600 people, but we had only sixteen present that day.

And yet she asked if she could come to my congregation in Park Slope. Mindy was far from God. She attended for a year, then brought along her boyfriend. They said they both wanted to be baptized. Both Mindy and the boyfriend became followers of Christ. Last week her mom friended me on Facebook." What began as a random meeting at a Reformed Church in Flatbush, Brooklyn, ended up with two people far from God being baptized in Park Slope, Brooklyn.

———|||———

100 LONG ISLAND CHURCH PLANTS
Brian McMillan and Revive Long Island

Hanging on Brian McMillan's Massapequa, Long Island, office wall is a full-length map of Long Island, including both Suffolk and Nassau Counties, which represents 3 million people. Long Island is ninety miles from the eastern border of Queens to the eastern tip that falls into the Atlantic Ocean by Montauk. This map has circles and pins indicating all the churches that represent what Brian would describe as "life giving." These are churches with strong biblical teaching and a commitment to community outreach. These churches are Baptist, Pentecostal, Nazarene, Episcopalian, Methodist, and everything in between.

McMillan is a gospel ecosystem thinker. He has built an incredible network of collaborative churches on Long Island. McMillan describes Long Island as "post Catholic" and "post Jewish," with about 3 percent of the Long Island population describing themselves as evangelical. Post Catholic and post Jewish means that families and individuals who were raised Catholic or Jewish have dropped out of church/synagogue and no longer practice their Catholicism/Judaism. "My vision for 2030 is to see a life-giving church in every one of the 191 zip codes on Long Island," he says. "That means that more than half of our zip codes need a new church."

When I arrived in Queens in 1984, for ten years I spent a great deal of time on Long Island for my InterVarsity responsibilities. During that time, I noticed that there was a huge dearth of growing and vibrant churches. While some dynamic churches existed, I did not find very many of them. However, in the late 1980s, Steve Tomlinson became pastor at Manhasset Baptist. Sensing a need to reintroduce the church to the community, Tomlinson led the church to a name change, Shelter Rock, and created a multi-site model. In two years, Shelter Rock grew 40 percent. It was a sign of a visionary, innovative leader. In that same spirit of innovation, Tomlinson and Brian McMillan and a few others began to work together to form Revive Long Island.

Revive Long Island wanted to address the isolation of pastors and churches. Its vision is to form friendships between leaders and to carve an identity as *one church* on Long Island.

McMillan recalls, "When I went into ministry at nineteen, I was alone, and no one befriended me. I want Revive Long Island to be a safe place that empowers leaders who become friends. We provide opportunities to gather for relationship and training. We also take on big projects that none of us could take on together. One project that is in early discussion is translating an entire Bible into a language together."

McMillan shared a powerful story of how churches are working together: "A small Baptist church in Babylon, Long Island, lost its senior pastor, Wayne Griffith, who died suddenly. They had been working with a young church plant led by Lou Pizzichillo. God orchestrated this tragic moment into something beautiful where a small church with a property merged with a young church plant with 200 attendees. This was something radical for Long Island and reflects the spirit of Revive Long Island."

Despite the challenges of expensive properties, McMillan believes that these are the best days to be leading on Long Island. "Every church that is theologically conservative, contemporary, and has a missional mindset is growing," he says. McMillan believes that if Revive Long Island can continue to grow, they will attract, train, and resource the 100 church planters needed to fulfill their Long Island 2030 vision of a vibrant church for every zip code there.

———╫———

"I WON'T CHARGE YOU A NICKEL, BUT IT WILL COST YOU YOUR LIFE."
Redd Sevilla Multiplies Missional Neighborhood Groups

One dimension of New York City's spiritual renaissance is the fruit of immigration from Latin America, Asia, and South America. This is true in the story of Redd Sevilla and his family.

Sevilla is an immigrant from the Philippines who landed in Queens as a young boy. His parents came to the United States to pursue the American dream, which soon became the American nightmare. "I came to the United States with my parents and three brothers," he says. "Sadly, my dad left my mom soon after we arrived. We had to fend for ourselves in New York City. Being undocumented immigrants did not make it easier. My mom had to work long hours for low pay to make ends meet. Adding to the stress was the fear of the government and deportation."

They met an accomplished corporate attorney from a Park Avenue law firm who said if they would trust her, she would not charge them the tens of thousands of dollars typically associated with any correction of immigration status. "She said she would work for us for free," he says. "We agreed. Who wouldn't? Having her by our side at no cost was a miracle!"

The prosecuting attorney had more than a dozen pieces of falsified documentation proving their illegal status and establishing criminal offense. In addition, the family could potentially be fined $400,000.

The Sevillas's attorney pled their case. As God would have it, Sevilla's mom had the foresight to pay taxes, even though she was undocumented and needed all the money she could get. Their judge was inspired by their mom's sacrifice and ruled in their favor, dismissing all fines. He also gave each of the Sevilla family members green cards, making them all eligible to remain in Queens.

This experience uniquely prepared Sevilla to lead at New Life Church in Elmhurst, Queens, one of the most ethnically diverse communities in the world.[8] He began his role in 2010 as the leader of the church's community-development corporation, New Life CDC, which has a health center that serves the under- and non-insured among immigrant families. New Life CDC offers seven other programs as a means of serving adults, youth, and children in the local neighborhood. They recognize that programs involved in food distribution, academic achievement, leadership development, and economic empowerment are means through which the love of God is demonstrated in word and deed.

In 2015, Sevilla saw a second miracle in the form of a vision. "I saw the two zip codes of Elmhurst and Corona covered in the dark sheet described in Isaiah 25:7. But then I saw the light of the gospel piercing the darkness. Imagine all 200,000 people from 150 nations in this neighborhood hearing the gospel!" The vision is to see four generations of followers of Jesus, based on 2 Timothy 2:2: "The things you have heard me say in the presence of many witnesses entrust to reliable people who will also be qualified to teach others."

That vision caused Sevilla and his wife, Aya, to research

effective means to reach more people and to have a disciple-making movement. His internet search led him to Steve Addison, who became an authorial mentor. Sevilla also met Bud Abbott, who offered to mentor him every week. When Sevilla asked him what it would cost, Bud responded, "I won't charge you a nickel, but it will cost you your life."

The call to generational multiplication soon became all consuming, and in 2016, Redd and Aya Sevilla began a house church model with nine other people (Peggy Liao, Vashti Gunness, Kit Yeung, Janice Tan, Jonjon and Jenny Mangahas, Kimberly Jones, and Dave and Vikki Padua) and called it a missional neighborhood group. By 2018, disciples were multiplying, and as people were converted to Christianity, they were baptized in bathtubs. That year, they home baptized thirteen people and baptized one person at a local park. Thirteen different people carried out the baptisms, demonstrating the multiplication of disciples.

The model played out in the story of Sevilla's leaders, Jonjon and Jenny. The three met weekly to hear the vision of Jesus in Matthew 28. As vision was cast, Jonjon reached out to a relative named David. Jonjon wound up baptizing David, who in turn reached out to a friend at work. David led the friend to Christ and baptized her at home in the presence of friends and her boyfriend.

The result of this season of fruitfulness? God is expanding his influence. Sevilla has been tasked with starting a new congregation in Nassau County, Long Island, where many New Life Fellowship leaders currently reside. As the result of this interview, I was able to introduce Brian McMillan (see Revive Long Island) and Sevilla to each other. The Kingdom is growing as the result of the ecosystem of relationships and vision.

Chapter 5

NEXT

My most formational spiritual experience took place in India in 1983, when I was twenty-four. My wife, Marya, and I traveled to North India for ten weeks with Operation Mobilization, a movement committed to evangelism and discipleship of young people across the globe. We were in Bihar, an Indian state with a population of 100 million people. The ratio of Muslims and Hindus to Christians was 100,000 to 1.

That summer we were shaped by a praying community that met every Friday for three to nine hours to implore God to act in this region of the world. We were also shaped by Mr. and Mrs. Chowdary, Hindu converts from Brahmin backgrounds, who led us through J. I. Packer's book *Knowing God* every week. Those ten weeks have shaped the last thirty-seven years.

The second most formative experience was selling our possessions and moving to New York City in June 1984, with InterVarsity, the campus organization I worked with for thirteen years. Leaving home with a three-month pregnant wife required an audacity of faith, which I had never experienced before. Within twelve months, our time in India and move to New York City taught us that every risk we take for God is transcended by His provision.

That all happened because the church saw my wife and me when we were young, and they fed into us a deep sense of purpose and significance. We could be part of something greater than ourselves, of work that God was doing! As we look at the second strategy for rejuvenating and changing the landscape of Christianity, my own experience validates that missions for young people is the most formational experience possible to ground their faith. And we, as church leaders, must pursue every opportunity to make this happen.

What We Need to Understand about Today's Young People

We make our greatest mistake if we believe young people— Millennials and Generation Z, those under the age of forty— are like we were when we were that age. If fact, today's young people are different from any other generation in history. Before we understand how to reach them and pour into their lives, we need to know more about who they are and what makes them tick.

According to Pew Research Center, "Millennials refer to those born between 1981–1996 and spread from post-college graduates to entry to mid-level workers. Generation Z refers to those born between 1997–2012 and straddle between elementary school and college at the stage of forming characters, world view, and beliefs. Millennials and Gen Z are tech-savvy. Gen Zers are true digital natives, born into internet/ Wi-Fi, and all sorts of digital gadgets (smart phones, laptops/

desktops, tables, gaming consoles, smart watches, and social media)."[1]

In *Faith for Exiles,* David Kinnaman and Mark Matlock explain that digital savvy in today's youth culture this way: "We at Barna have adopted a phrase to describe our complex, accelerated culture that is marked by phenomenal access, profound alienation, and a crisis of authority as *digital Babylon.*"[2] This digital Babylon expresses itself in this way, according to Luke Greenwood in *Global Youth Culture*: "The current urban generation connected by consumerism, social media, and the entertainment industry forms the largest global culture to ever exist.[3] The existing world view for many young people is desperate, arrogant, and vacant. A postmodern world view puts man at the center which results in these expressions of that world view."[4]

And we see them respond to that view by yearning for something more, something significant. Two of the top concerns for these two generations are climate change and income inequality. Their body of concerns also includes animal rights, sustainability of the economy, environmental protection, anti-racism, inclusiveness, feminism, and LGBTQ rights.[5] In other words, if we look at what younger people say they value, it becomes clear that young people have a passion for equality and their own futures. Only in Jesus and the gospel will their quest be addressed for their immediate good and the good of the world. The best way to steward our lives and the planet is to grasp God's redemptive work in us and through us.

We also need to understand the influence these two generations wield. Why? Simply put, when the Baby Boomers arrived on the scene, they were the largest generation in history. Their sheer numbers pushed a fundamental shift in the way the world acted and perceived life. The Millennials and Generation Z have even bigger numbers. According to Al Miyashita, leader of the Millennial Working Group, "In the United States the Millennial and Generation Z together are already the largest population of all the previous generations. The Millennial generation alone is 72 million and entering their prime working years. The Generation Z is closely following. These two generations are quite different in their perspectives, their wants, and desires, their interactions, and how they do things. The one thing we know is that these are the most un-churched generations and consequently they will affect our government, businesses, communities, and the world. It is imperative that we make inroads into these generations with the gospel in hopes of transforming the future of the world."[6]

And where do we find most of them? In *Global Youth Culture,* Luke Greenwood observes that "around 54 percent of the world population currently lives in urban centers. That is nearly 4 billion people. The 2 billion young people in this setting, part of the Global Youth Culture, I have described have little chance of hearing who Jesus is. Two billion people."[7] As we consider New York City's population, it is estimated that we have 2 million young people ages eighteen and under living here.[8]

We have our work cut out for us. As we look to the second strategy of impacting New York City—and ultimately the entire world—with the gospel, we must set our eyes toward evangelistically reaching the 2 million young people ages eighteen and younger of New York City and grounding them in a lifetime of fruitful discipleship. In other words, we must respond to who they are and how they tick by understanding them and then giving them the answers they long for.

How Do We Respond?

So how do we do that? How do we reach 2 million young people and pour into them the significance that they are ultimately yearning for? How do we counteract the digital Babylon with the truth and power of the gospel? The New York City Millennial Work Group believes we can impact 275,000 young people over this next decade, and they have some strategies on how to accomplish it.

The New York City Millennial Work Group is a community of leaders with a common passion to impact the next generation. It is made up of a powerful ecosystem of talented leaders and organizations with decades of presence in New York City, including Al Miyashita, Peter Trautmann, and Steve Tice from The Navigators, Colin Nykaza from the Catholic Archdiocese, Jessica Toussaint from Bridges to Promise, Keller Rudsill and Francis Floth from Cru, Jason Gaboury from InterVarsity, Matt Perman from The King's College, Emily Wang from Stevens Institute, Jeremy Del Rio from Thrive Collective, Maurice Winley from Living Redemption, and Paul Coty from Young Life.[9]

In the context of New York City, they have identified two primary strategies to impact and empower young people:

High School Chapters

One strategy is to see Young Life open new chapters in public schools. After the New York City Board of Education announced it would no longer provide any after-school programming beginning with the 2020–2021 school year, Young Life saw an opportunity to start new chapters as after-school options. Currently Young Life is impacting 10,000 young people in their campus work in twenty-two community districts in

New York City. With this new approach they could potentially grow their reach to 100,000 young people in all fifty-nine community districts by 2026.

Young Life can interface with churches like New Life and the Coalition of Youth Pastors to identify young leaders attending these schools. The Coalition of Youth Pastors represents more than 100 churches in New York City that meet every quarter for training under the direction of Adam Durso, executive director of LEAD.NYC. They work to identify leaders to help plant chapters for both Young Life and Navigator Bible Clubs.

At the university level, InterVarsity, Cru, and The Navigators all have significant presence on dozens of universities in the region. The strategy is to create a more robust pipeline of young people from high school into university ministries.

Business and Entrepreneurship

The second strategy is to influence at-risk youth by creating entrepreneurial and business opportunities for them through mentoring intensive programming. The pipeline here is to direct young people currently participating in schools attached to Thrive Collective led by Jeremy Del Rio (see his story in this chapter) toward Living Redemption and Praxis for their at-risk youth mentoring programs.

Thrive Collective currently has influence in 200 schools in New York City participating in art education and mentoring. The students are 83 percent ethnic minority (see Paul Coty's story in this chapter). The students are great candidates, given their willingness to participate in programming for significant mentoring opportunities and employment training.

Two of Thrive Collective's collaborative partners are Praxis and Living Redemption. Praxis is a creative engine for redemptive entrepreneurship, supporting founders, funders, and innovators motivated by their faith to renew culture and love their neighbors. Its community of practice operates through high-touch programs, robust content, and a global portfolio of redemptive business and nonprofit ventures.

Living Redemption (see Maurice Winley's story in this chapter) is a mentoring program for at-risk youth with roots in Harlem. They currently impact 300 students as the result of grants they have received from the city. The critical success factor in this strategy is the trust level between the leaders of these organizations and their commitment to work in a coordinated manner that allows successful introductions. Living Redemption and Praxis prepare young people for future employment, which is illustrated by training in the hospitality industry.

Disciplining the Next Generation for Lifetime Fruitfulness

I have been privileged to work with young people in their late teens entering university and seeing their maturation over thirty years. One of my favorite stories is that of Dr. Joe Cina, whom I met at Polytechnic University in Brooklyn in the late 1980s. Cina became active in the InterVarsity Christian Fellowship group, which we planted together. He came from an immigrant family, earned his PhD in physics, and has been an extraordinary model in the marketplace of integrating faith and work. His oldest daughter is now beginning her college experience. Our investment in younger leaders has generational fruitfulness.

In their book *Faith for Exiles,* Kinnaman and Matlock have summarized their research about resilient discipleship for the next generation. They have identified five practices that cause young people to be fruitful:

1. They form a resilient identity. When they experience *intimacy with Jesus,* they are transformed.
2. They develop muscles of cultural discernment (wisdom), which allows them to stand firm in a complex and anxious age.
3. Where isolation and mistrust are the norms, they forge meaningful, intergenerational relationships.
4. They are grounded and motivated, and train for vocational discipleship.
5. They curb their entitlement and self-centered tendencies by engaging in cross-cultural mission.[10]

Kinnaman writes, "Teens are most interested in joining missions when it will cost everything. Undertaking a radical life altering mission is what this generation craves."[11] The relationship between intimacy with Jesus and mission with Jesus is inextricable. As we mentioned in chapter 2, the Mormon church is exceedingly effective with the next generation. It is not accidental that Mormon young people are expected to serve in one-to-two-year mission projects before college, which results in a depth of commitment to their faith. Mormons also have a high family value, which reflects on intergenerational relationships. They are intentional in pouring into their youth. We must be as well.

Specifically, what should happen?

We need to return to a catechism training—religious education—within both our homes and our churches. To that end,

Redeemer Presbyterian Church has created "The New City Cat-echism Devotional," which guides families through fifty-two questions to help young people become grounded in what we believe.[12]

We must also explore new catechistic expressions that bet-ter communicate with the next generation. For instance, if this generation is about technology, then we go to them and speak in their language of technology. Kinnaman writes that to form wisdom within young people, we must "instill and transmit cultural discernment in digital Babylon, faith communities and households [to] become robust learning communities."[13] Where there are stable families who have a relationship with the gospel, this is of paramount importance.

The Fuller Youth Institute (FYI), a close partner with Barna and with Pinetops Foundation, has a vision to train 100,000 churches on increasing their youth discipleship effectiveness with best practices—and they want to make New York City one of the discipleship training hubs by leveraging the Youth Pas-tors Coalition (YPC). In this context, FYI and the YPC can use curricula like *Faith for Exiles* to motivate more effective disci-pleship among New York City churches.

Creating Youth on Mission

One of the great needs is to scale the awareness and opportu-nities for young people to participate in radical, life-forming mission experiences. Experiences can happen inside New York City, impoverished areas within the United States (such as Appalachia), or overseas. One of my observations from work-ing with college students for thirteen years is that an experience needs to be concentrated enough in a person's life for a behavior to change. That experience could be a missions conference like Urbana for college students, or a mission trip of one to twelve weeks.

Some of the best resources for missions training are with East West, a Dallas-based missions group working throughout the United States and in dozens of countries (eastwest.org). Since their founding, East West leaders have shared the gospel with nearly 200 million people and planted nearly 200,000 churches. East West introduces young people and lay people to powerful, life-altering mission opportunities.

Another solid organization doing similar work is Touch the World, a New Jersey-based organization that offers mission trips to fourteen locations within the United States and globally (touchtheworld.org).

The Most Important Thing

The sum of all of this is simple. The most important thing that can happen globally is to reach young people in big cities. That is the bullseye. That is the ball game. As we stated in chapter 1, the scale of our fruitfulness will be determined by the strength of our collective commitment to each other in the gospel eco-system to reach the next generation.

"GO GET MY BABIES"
Paul Coty and the Story of Young Life NYC

If we are serious about growing and empowering the church in the next decade, we must be serious and urgent about impacting young people with the gospel. No other organization in New York City is impacting more young people than Young Life under the leadership of Paul Coty.

Coty is the vice president of the Northeast Atlantic Subdivision for Young Life. He has twenty years' experience in the multiethnic ministry landscape and is one of the most effective leaders in the globe at strategically reaching young people in the urban setting.

Coty, an African American, grew up in Iowa where the African-American population is 3.5 percent. "I was an eleven-year-old gangly kid. I felt awkward and without much significance," he says. He was shaped, poured into, and greatly influenced by a church named Gospel Tabernacle, a woman named Evangelist Mary Beets, and a group of godly men. Mary Beets "called me her little preacher man," he says. "She created a youth service and the youth ran everything. She molded me as a young Christian." Coty's spiritual foundation was laid. And then that group of men built upon it: one man developed Coty's understanding of God's Word, another shaped his relationships with the opposite sex, another facilitated his relationship with money, another shaped his thinking around major decisions, and the last one helped him develop godly character in times of crisis. "Without this community when I was young, I would not be the same person," he says.

Coty had heard of Young Life, as his mother was a board member of the chapter in Cedar Rapids, Iowa. He then was introduced to the ministry of Young Life during the summer of 1997 and became a staff member in the summer of 1999. He arrived in New York City in 2003 to be part of the emerging Young Life strategy to reach young people in the twelve-to-twenty-two age range. Coty's background as a minority in Iowa helped give him the cross-cultural agility to work in the context of New York City.

In 2009 Young Life announced an ambitious community district plan. At that time Young Life was working with 1,000 young people in four community districts. In 2020, with their staff team of forty-two, their impact is now reaching 9,800 young people in twenty-two community districts. This is nearly a 1,000 percent increase in a decade. But for them, that's just the beginning. "Our new vision is to be present in all fifty-nine community districts by 2026 and impacting 100,000 young people," he says. New York City has more than 1 million young people in school in those community districts. The ethnic breakdown in NYC public schools is:

41 percent Hispanic
26 percent African American
16 percent Asian

15 percent White

2 percent Other[14]

Why is this breakdown important? "Young people of color suffer from a lack of hope because there is such a profound lack of opportunity," he says. "Most young people cannot pay for college. We see an increase in suicide as young people get in trouble and can't find a way out." As an antidote to that hopelessness, Young Life has broadened its outreach from middle school through college and broadened its scope to include programs for teen moms and young people with special needs.

Speaking to what was so critical to their remarkable growth, Coty said, "We see ourselves in the picture. We have recruited adults of color and empowered them to reach young people of color." He is also amazed by the supernatural way God has brought leaders onto their team, including staff member Aswan Morris. Coty met Morris in 2003 at a church basketball league. Morris was a talented athlete and a burgeoning businessman. They grew their friendship as Coty met with Morris for breakfast every Wednesday. Coty asked him if he ever considered youth ministry. Morris responded, "I don't do that." Yet slowly Morris began to express interest in Coty's invitation.

When Morris was offered a $70,000 contract to play basketball with the American Basketball Association, Coty concluded there was no way Morris would consider walking away from that contract to join the Young Life team. And yet he did. When Coty asked him what made the difference, Morris replied that he had asked God what he should do. God spoke to Morris, *Go get my babies.*

Morris joined the Young Life staff and has been an instrumental force in the growth of Young Life New York City. God has breathed on Young Life New York City because of their collective will to provide the Lord's "babies" a future and a hope.

———†††———

WHERE A MOMENT BECOMES A MEMORY
Jeremy Del Rio and Thrive Collective
Impacting 500 Schools

One of the themes of *The Great Opportunity* is to be more engaged in the public square to create long-term witness. Jeremy Del Rio has embodied this for twenty years through his engagement in New York University as a student and now as an advocate for under-resourced public school students.

Del Rio grew up the son of a preacher. His parents, Rick and Arlene, planted themselves in the 1980s in the Lower East Side of Manhattan in a neighborhood filled with drugs and gangs. Del Rio learned at an early age what it means to be called to the gritty communities of New York.

Del Rio preached his first sermon at age thirteen. He started a youth group at the age of nineteen. When he attended New York University, he led its InterVarsity group. That was where Del Rio and I first met. And in our twenty years of knowing and working together, he has been undoubtedly one of the most effective and collaborative leaders I have worked with.

And yet his journey did not take a direct, though assumed,

route into the ministry. "I felt led to be more of a prophet than a preacher," he says. "That is why I went to law school rather than seminary. I feel drawn to the biblical characters of Joseph, Daniel, and Esther. They made their difference in the public square."

From there he founded Thrive Collective, which offers art education and mentoring to some of the 250,000 students in the New York City public school system currently without access to art education. One of the fruits of that educational experience is that the students paint a mural on the walls of their schools. Del Rio's team has helped students complete 135 murals with 60 in process, which cover 60,000 square feet of public school space.

Del Rio says, "We are providing students the opportunity to experience the first fruit of Scripture, the opportunity to create. It is how young people discover their *Imago Dei*. As the result of our work, the doors of public schools are opening to faith groups like Young Life and others. Our work is helping to fill the gaps for the 419 schools that have lost art education."

In 2008 Del Rio helped our team launch The New York City Leadership Center at the Cornell Club in Manhattan with a presentation on "2020: A Vision for New York City Public Schools." This was his first collaborative partnership for NYCLC. "Twenty twenty was a rhetorical device to draw attention to the underserved student population of New York City," he says. "Now that we are in 2020, we look back and see our impact in 200 of the 1,800 public schools providing art education and mentoring for 50,000 students. This is growth from the first 3,000 students we were working with in 2010. We believe that through art, young people have a moment that becomes a lasting memory."

As for his decadal vision, he admits, "We want to be in 30 percent of the public schools in New York City by 2030 (540 schools), and in 10 percent of the US cities that are larger than 100,000 people. We want to see an ecosystem of artists that can help each other incubate careers. This meets an enormous felt need to provide a future hope for young people of color in our cities."

ANSWERING THE CALL FROM STREET UNIVERSITY TO MINISTER OF THE GOSPEL
Maurice Winley and Credible Messenger Movement

Maurice Winley was privileged to grow up in a Christian home in Harlem. His father is a second-generation pastor at the Soul Saving Station, a revered Harlem church. Winley attended private school before entering Jamaica High School.

His goal was to become a doctor. But something happened that changed the course of his life. When he was seventeen, during a homeroom session, he was involved in a shooting that ended another student's life. This tragedy, in addition to a series of events and circumstances that followed, made an indelible psychological impact on Winley. It caused him, he says, to enroll in "Street University." That choice led to Winley being sentenced to the State Department of Corrections and spending time in Rikers Island.

After he served his time, while at work managing two stores selling compact discs, one day a man entered one of the stores and attempted a robbery. Winley shot and killed the assailant. Winley found himself in front of a grand jury with a new charge that carried a sentence of twenty-five years to life. Before the trial began, the victim's mother confronted Winley. Her words were so powerful that he experienced what he calls "a horror of conscience." He deeply regretted his act and vowed to the court that if he was given a second chance, he would dedicate his life to helping other young men from going down a destructive path.

While he awaited his trial, he returned to the church seeking forgiveness, but he was also prepared to be sentenced. During a sermon his father, Robert Winley, gave, Winley rededicated his life to the Lord. On the day he was to appear for court, his father prayed a simple prayer over him, that God would judge his heart.

Miraculously, after his testimony, the judge threw out the case. Winley's resolve to re-surrender his life to God was also his call to impact vulnerable young men, particularly of African-American and Latino descent.

In 2001, as that call on his life and ministry matured, Winley became involved with The Navigators under the mentorship of Andy Puleo, who served as the organization's NYC director. What impressed Winley was that Puleo was authentic, intentional, relentless in discipling, and a servant leader. Winley credits Puleo's influence on his philosophy of ministry, with an emphasis on life-on-life discipleship, to the successes he has experienced as a leader and mentor. "He exemplified it in how he lived," Winley says.

Puleo also affirmed Winley's call and helped him synthesize the mission and vision for the movement God had placed on his heart. "As a movement leader, Puleo was excited when he learned of my one-on-one interactions, and that encouraged me."

Puleo's investment of time discipling and mentoring him, along with the significant relationships that came through Winley's involvement with The Navigators, became a perpetual source of inspiration and encouragement. Winley also attributes his training with The Navigators to him seeing discipleship as a leadership paradigm that fosters leadership replication. In the traditional church environment Winley grew up in, discipleship was assumed versus modeled, he says. Hence, his ministry connection with Puleo and The Navigators was God-orchestrated. "The Navigators became an oasis in my wilderness of discovering, hearing, and responding to God's call," he says.

Another influential leader in Winley's life was Jack Crabtree, who served as executive director of Long Island Youth for Christ, and who shared many structural insights and tools with Winley, which deepened his paradigm of ministry.

Winley's leadership arc began as a chaplain at Saint Christopher Inc., an adolescent residential treatment center, and his role later expanded to director of spiritual life and positive youth development, providing services to three residential campuses and four high schools. His passion to impact justice-involved youth and community engagement grew over the years. Under Mayor Bloomberg's administration, in 2012, Winley was awarded one of nineteen contracts to launch the ARCHES Transformative Mentoring Program in Harlem, and was recognized as the top site across the five boroughs. The distinguishing element of his Harlem site was discipling and building a family among gang leaders. "The secret sauce is one-on-one, life-on-life discipleship."

Due to the ARCHES' success, Winley received the opportunity to be a cofounder of the Credible Messenger Justice Center, which disseminates best practices around criminal justice systems and community partnerships around the country. This led to opportunities to speak at monthly reentry forums, which in turn led to a collaborative initiative called Clean Slate, in which the Manhattan DA's office sent letters to 2,000 individuals with low-level crimes on their record with the offer to have their records expunged if they came to a gathering at the Soul Saving Station on November 21, 2015. Winley saw 800 people come forward to receive a clean slate.

In February 2017, Winley, along with four other organizations, received individual grants to implement five "Youth Opportunity Hubs" throughout Manhattan. Winley launched Living Redemption Youth Opportunity Hub in July 2017 to serve the youth and young adults of Central and West Harlem, which he leads as founder and executive director.

Winley knows that the Credible Messenger Movement model works and has proven results. "The entry point is trauma," he says. "We are data driven, and our model is scalable. In the ARCHES Transformative Mentoring program, for example, based on a five-year evaluation of all the young people we mentored while they were on probation, 68 percent did not reoffend." Winley continues to expand his vision to reach more justice-impacted youth and communities, and has broadened his scope and vision to be a catalyst for the Credible Messenger Movement in cities such as Washington DC, Philadelphia, Atlanta, Houston, San Diego, Chicago, and throughout the Greater Capital Region of New York. "We want to become a movement that will generate movements."

━━━━ ╫ ━━━━

DISCIPLING THE NATIONS IN THE NEXT GENERATION
Matt Manno and the New Life Model

When churches and faith organizations work intentionally to disciple young people, those young people have a long-term trajectory in their faith. The necessity to be deeply grounded in the truths of Christianity is paramount. This is something New Life, a Queens congregation under the leadership of Matt Manno, knows well.

Manno grew up at First Baptist Church of Flushing, part of the diverse congregation that represents sixty language groups. He understands diversity, as his father, Sal, is Italian, and his mom, Veronica, is African American. The leaders in the church challenged Manno, and the other young people in church, to seek their true identity in Jesus. Manno explains that "the greatest challenge facing every young person is 'Who am I? Do I belong?' Every young person is on a quest to discover who they are. They get conflicting messages where they fit in." Manno was no exception.

Manno's journey as he matured through leadership in the First Baptist youth group was to land full time at New Life Church in Elmhurst, Queens. Pete Scazzero, author of *Emotionally Healthy Spirituality,* founded New Life with its 1,200 attendees. Like First Baptist of Flushing, New Life is in one of the most ethnically diverse neighborhoods in the world. The church has seventy-five nationalities. Scazzero believes that the frontier for discipleship is emotional maturity. He says that you cannot be spiritually mature and emotionally immature. He has spoken this message on six continents to thousands of leaders.

The vision for New Life is not just to reach young people but to ground them in a lifetime of emotionally healthy discipleship that will allow them to be fruitful for life. Manno says, "My calling is to be involved with teenagers. The vision for discipleship has to be broadened to care for the entire family." Of the 1,200 attendees at New Life, 600 fall into Manno's realm of responsibility as the Next Generation pastor, which includes discipling young people and their families.

Through Manno's leadership, he places a strong emphasis on creating a contemplative spirituality for young people, which provides space to reflect on God's work in young people's lives and how it expresses itself emotionally and in family.

Manno says that small groups are the core methodology of disciplining young people. He has created safe peer groups where young people can disclose themselves without fear of judgment. He has seen the impact on a young woman who had a consistent adult in her life. Her journey took her from a stage of insecurity to becoming one of the main worship leaders in her church. As her spiritual life deepened, she learned to embrace God's love for her.

Manno's decadal vision is to see great collaboration between churches and agencies with a common vision to disciple young people into emotional and spiritual health. Manno concludes, "Growing large is not nearly as important as developing young people of depth."

THE BIBLE AND THE PUBLIC SCHOOL
Ernie Scalabrin Plants Bible Clubs

Emerging from World War II, one of the great disciple-making movements is The Navigators. The thrust of The Navigators ministry began with teaching the Bible and Scripture memorization to soldiers. Today it is a multiethnic, global ministry on college campuses and in churches, prisons, neighborhoods, public schools, the military, cities, and the marketplace, in which they continue to place strong emphasis on God's Word.

Ernie Scalabrin's life intersected with The Navigators thirty-nine years ago at Rutgers University, when he accepted Christ. He became impacted deeply by the life-on-life discipleship ministry of The Navigators. "I was shown early the importance of daily devotions, the study of Scripture, and how to apply it daily to life," he says. "I also learned that no matter where I worked, that was my mission field."

Scalabrin taught in public schools for twelve years in nearby Elizabeth, New Jersey. Like many other inner-city New Jersey communities, its population has a high density of minorities and immigrants. While there, he helped create an effective after-school student mentoring ministry based on Isaiah 58:12

called "Restore." He found that whether it was teaching for twelve years in school or now with The Navigators on staff for twenty-five years, the mission is the same: "to know Christ and to make Him known, helping others do the same."

A great opportunity emerged in 2001 after the Equal Access laws were enacted regarding public schools. With this new open door, Scalabrin began to teach, lead, train volunteers, and plant Bible clubs in schools. For him and his growing Navigator volunteer teaching team, it has become a web of opportunity to lead scores of children, grades kindergarten through twelfth, to Christ, and to disciple them and their families, as well as to influence school staff.

Scalabrin talks about this crucially important stage of a person's life: "Barna research states that 60 percent of faith commitments are made by children between the ages of four to fourteen. By the age of sixteen, the percentage is 85 percent." The vision is to plant Bible clubs that can freely share the gospel and disciple through every educational level—elementary, middle school, and high school across America. As this is a relatively new effort, Scalabrin is pleased that they have Bible clubs present in eight schools currently in New Jersey with a plan to be in twelve schools by 2021. The vision is to reach at least 100 schools over the next decade. The Bible club methodology is a great companion to the work of the other agencies—Young Life, Thrive Collective, and Living Redemption.

Scalabrin sees that the greatest challenges depend on the age group. For younger children, it is helping them to become consistent in their daily devotions and Scripture memory. For older children, it is competing with sports schedules. Yet he remains encouraged. In the 2018–2019 school year alone, seventy-one children professed faith commitments. Scalabrin is seeing open doors not just with students but with faculty, custodial, and other staff in schools. He is also seeing more churches getting involved with his Bible clubs for greater community outreach.

Scalabrin feels that the best antidote to young people walking away from their faith (see chapter 3) is by grounding them in the Bible with Scripture memorization. He also emphasizes teaching apologetics, which answers today's ever-increasing intellectual challenges to faith, especially given that, according to Barna, 70 percent of evangelical youth will walk away from their faith after high school. Ultimately, he recognizes that a sustained movement of God in a younger generation will need to be grounded in effective, life-changing disciplines of Scripture study.

Chapter 6

MARGINS

In February 1996 I was on holiday when I picked up Jonathan Kozol's book *Amazing Grace*. The book is a sweeping analysis of the plight of children in the South Bronx community of Mott Haven. I was hooked as soon as I read the first paragraph: "The Number 6 train from Manhattan to the South Bronx makes nine stops in the 18-minute ride between East 59th Street and Brook Avenue. When you enter the train, you are in the seventh richest congressional district in the nation. When you leave, you are in the poorest."[1]

Perhaps that paragraph captures the chasm of rich and poor in New York City as well as has ever been written. What makes the reality of the poor even more devastating is that they are also largely invisible, which further marginalizes them from society. According to Chris Whitford, CEO of Avail NYC, "Marginalization represents things we don't want to pay attention to. We want to get those persons or situations out of our vision, those conversations that cause our worldview to fall short."[2]

As I write this chapter, New York City—in fact, the entire

country—is engulfed in two major catastrophes: COVID-19 and the riots following the death of George Floyd, a man who died directly after a police officer in Minneapolis knelt on his neck for more than nine minutes, asphyxiating him. The faith community has an important moment in the history of our nation to respond with empathy and engagement in the plight of those who have been disadvantaged and discriminated against.

God has called us to care for those less advantaged. As Josh Crossman states in his opening paragraph on care for the poor in *The Great Opportunity*, "Care for the poor and oppressed is an essential and inescapable element of the Gospel message. It is pervasive and consistent in the Old and New Testaments. It was the witness of the early church and indeed the church throughout the last 2,000 years. Can it be any surprise, then, that historically the church has flourished during seasons of sacrificial service to the least of these?"[3]

Caring for the poor is at the heart of the gospel and manifests Jesus' love for the most vulnerable. So as we look to 2030, striving to reach and influence more people for the gospel, one of our missions is to pursue the opportunities we have in caring for marginalized people.

Poverty's Edge

In chapter 2 we looked at the historic impact of many agencies to the marginalized, particularly in the 1865–1920 period. New York City has a rich history of embracing the poor. Today is no different. New York City has an extraordinary community of leaders and agencies currently who comprise an ecosystem of agencies that are engaging those who are marginalized.

Given the environment we are all leading in, it is imperative that the ecosystem mature to take on the greatest challenges facing the hardest-hit communities, which are those in poverty.

We typically see an inverse relationship between affluence and spiritual receptivity. The more affluent a society, the less that society feels a need for God. The poor more easily understand how dependent they are on God. It is especially true in New York City where communities of color are most disadvantaged economically and educationally, even as they are far more spiritually engaged than Anglo Christians. And yet despite the great challenges facing us, we can be assured that God will use our sustained efforts to draw marginalized people to Himself in extraordinary numbers.

To understand the challenge of poverty in New York City, consider that from NYC's population of 8.7 million,[4] 43 percent live at or near the poverty line.[5] That represents approximately 3.7 million people. And those are pre-COVID/pre-riots numbers.

In the post-COVID environment, churches and agencies will need to think and act differently to navigate all the new economic challenges facing their constituents. It will require new innovations. For example, our team put together a proposal with nine partners to assist two zip codes in creating technology hubs for young people with limited access to the internet. Without adequate internet access, young people in poorer communities fall further behind as they cannot participate in distance learning.

Yet we have already seen a remarkable recent history of innovation to serve the poor in New York City. In 1986, under the leadership of Preston Washington, Harlem Congregations for Community Improvement (HCCI) was organized to address the need for affordable housing. In 1987, 64 percent of the families in Harlem had annual incomes of less than $10,000 and only 8 percent had incomes of more than $25,000. Since 1970, Central Harlem's population declined by one-third. Given the lack of opportunity, many citizens left depressed neighborhoods, leaving only those who were unable to afford a move, which meant the community grew even poorer.[6]

Under Washington's leadership, 100 congregations, including a mosque and a synagogue, developed a partnership with Mayor Dinkins' administration (1990–1993). The fruit of that partnership was the building of $200 million in affordable housing and the incubation of services for the community, including technology for young people to learn marketable skills. HCCI provided services and counseling resources for those with HIV/AIDS, among numerous others.

Hope for New York, under the leadership of Esther Larson, is another model of innovative leadership to address the issues of poverty and injustice in New York City. Their vision and mission: "Our vision is a New York City in which all people experience spiritual, social, and economic flourishing through the demonstration of Christ's love. Our mission is to mobilize volunteer and financial resources to support non-profit organizations serving the poor and marginalized in New York City."[7]

In 2019, Hope for New York distributed $2.3 million in grants to support affiliate organizations and mobilized nearly 35,000 volunteer hours. Hope for New York partners with fifty local agencies engaged with the poor. They are accelerating the ecosystem of agencies working together by linking them through financial grants and volunteers. One affiliate is All Angels Church, an Episcopal congregation on the Upper West Side of Manhattan, through meals, addiction services, and Sunday services.

A sister initiative is the Rescue Alliance, under the leadership of Brian Moll. Rescue Alliance has a rich, if but contemporary, history of working in New York City: "Our history began ten years ago as a yearly outreach to people living on the street during the peak of New York's brutal winter. Each February, committed volunteers equipped by the original founding organizations, walk every block of our city, and bring hope to our friends on the street. What began as an event has sparked a movement as everyone involved dreamed about collaborating to provide year-round compassionate, comprehensive care in response to the growing crisis of homelessness."[8]

Rescue Alliance finds its roots in the century-old legacy of faith-based outreach to homeless New Yorkers on Manhattan's Lower East Side by the New York City Rescue Mission and The Bowery Mission, two of the oldest gospel rescue missions and founders of a movement of more than 300 faith-based organizations across the United States.

In the modern era, as the factors leading to homelessness have shifted, Rescue Alliance members continue to respond to the call to reach out and develop consistent, ongoing relationships with people living without adequate housing. NYC Relief Bus goes out every day to distribute hot meals, hygiene kits, and other tangible resources through mobile outreach and case management. The Salvation Army, The Bowery Mission, New York City Rescue Mission, and Goodwill Rescue Mission offer emergency shelter, compassionate care, and residential life-transformation programs. This work is fueled by the support of Hope for New York, mobilizing volunteer and financial resources to serve the poor and marginalized in New York City."[9]

These extraordinary agencies represent a mature ecosystem of friendship making a massive difference in New York City among the poor. The Rescue Alliance model is a best practice that every city of the world can easily replicate. It is not coincidental that the growth of Christianity in Manhattan by 300 percent (see chapter 1) parallels the last twenty-five years of compassionate care for the poor. God has breathed on the heroic efforts of churches and agencies by making the gospel attractive through care for the poor. We believe through our concerted efforts in this area, more marginalized people will become attracted to the church as we move toward 2030.

Challenges Facing the Compassionate Movement

Mother Teresa reminds us that Jesus is in His most distressing disguise in the poor.[10] The poor often emerge from broken families and broken communities. I remember a tour through South Dallas with a pastor, Chris Simmons, who told me 97 percent of the children in his community were fatherless. He called it the cradle-to-prison pipeline.

According to Ed Morgan, chairman emeritus of The Bowery Mission, the root cause of homelessness is fatherlessness: "In 1965, Senator Daniel Moynihan stated that the root cause of poverty was the breakup of the family. At that time 8 percent of the families in the country had experienced breaking up. Moynihan said that 15 percent would change society. Today 41 percent of all births are out of wedlock, including 70 percent in the minority community. Nationally there are 500,000 homeless, which follows the curve with out-of-wedlock births."[11]

In recent months we have seen an explosion of homelessness in West Coast cities. Morgan, who serves as a consultant to the national rescue movement, sees these homelessness trends with great alarm. He stresses that the real root issue for homelessness is loss of family and community. According to Morgan, we have not succeeded in America by effectively bringing together the three-legged stool of the for-profit community, the nonprofit community, and the government. And worse for us is that the poor are in our churches, just not made to feel part of the church community. Something we must change.

What We Can Do to Respond

In Matthew 25, Jesus reminds us that our engagement with the poor and the prisoner is a mirror of our spirituality. The 2,000 verses of Scripture that point toward the poor and marginalized speak to the priority and urgency of engaging those less fortunate. Our engagement with the poor validates our faith to a watching world. So how must we respond to Christ's call to care for the poor and introduce them to the Good News? We start with the following:

Recommendation #1: Engage God's Heart for the Poor

We need to understand God's heart for the poor. Only then can we truly succeed in our evangelistic efforts with them. Proverbs 19:17 says, "Whoever is kind to the poor lends to the LORD." It is important to read the Bible through the lens of what it says about the poor. Prayer and philanthropy are two immediate ways to engage. My wife and I sponsor twenty-four children in Africa and Haiti through World Vision. Our connection to these children keeps our hearts tender toward them and their communities.

Recommendation #2: Study the Plight of the Poor

Become more educated on the current plight of the poor. It is important to build a reading list that provides greater depth of understanding of the marginalized and what we can do to enter their worlds. Foundational reading includes *Rich Christians in an Age of Hunger* by Ron Sider, *Whole in the Gospel* by Rich Stearns, and *Theirs Is the Kingdom* by Robert Lupton. I also strongly recommend taking day tours of your city with skillful guides who understand the history of disadvantaged neighborhoods. Make it a priority to build a relationship with persons who have greater needs than yourself.

Recommendation #3: Consider Your and Your Congregation's Posture

Assess your own congregation and its posture toward the poor. What can you do to create a more welcoming environment and pathway into the center of community? Is there overt effort to invite economically challenged persons in your community to join your congregation and then include them?

Recommendation #4: Volunteer

Get involved. You can find tremendous opportunities in New York City to volunteer with the agencies mentioned in this chapter: Avail NYC (availnyc.org); The Bowery Mission (Bowery.org); Hope for New York (HFNY.org); Rescue Alliance (Rescuealliance.org); Youth for Christ (YFC.net); New York City Relief (reliefbus.org); and LEAD.NYC (lead.nyc).

Recommendation #5: Scale a Collaborative Model

For those with time and financial capacity, invest in agencies that are doing great work. Contact any of the agencies we have highlighted here to explore avenues of financial engagement. These agencies are multipliers. The leaders of The Bowery Mission believe, for instance, that a $20,000 investment through their residency program can change a life forever.

IO ZIP CODES
Adam Durso and LEAD.NYC Pioneer the Effort to Impact Marginalized Young People

In 1996, Adam Durso's parents, Mike and Maria, had a dual challenge. Their first challenge was that their oldest son, Adam, was at college and far from God. Their second challenge was that their church, Christ Tabernacle, in Glendale, Queens, drew 500 adults but had an anemic youth group with only eighteen young people. How could they influence their son to accept Christ when he was uninterested in church or the things of God? So Maria committed to pray and fast for Adam's salvation.

Miraculously and powerfully, Adam came to faith thanks in great part to his mother's fasting and prayers.

His faith became so real to him that he immediately wanted others to experience the same thing. But looking at their youth group's ministry, he knew they could do better.

With the church leaders' permission, Adam took charge of the youth group and reformatted it to be more contemporary with hip-hop music and youthful speakers. He also renamed the youth group to Youth Explosion. Soon it attracted more and more young people, until the group began averaging between 500 and 700 young people every Friday night, becoming the largest youth group in New York City. Every Friday night, young people lined up around the block to join the event.

At the end of each meeting, the leaders invited the youth to participate in an altar call for them to surrender their lives to Jesus. Next to the altar sat a large plexiglass box where young people deposited anything that had been a spiritual hindrance in their lives—drugs, knives, and even expensive tennis shoes. The impact of Youth Explosion was so palpable that the local police precinct noticed the decline in youth criminal activity. The youth group planted within Durso an enormous passion to reach young people living in vulnerable neighborhoods, such as the ones surrounding the church.

Having served on the church's leadership team since 1996, in 2017, Durso felt it was time to move into a broader ministry and accepted the position of executive director of LEAD. NYC, the New York City expression of Movement.org. Collaborating with the Cinnamon Network from the United Kingdom, Durso's team surveyed the poorest communities in New York City to define their greatest needs and to see how the organization could best meet them.

In their research they found four common factors facing these communities: (1) high prevalence of teen pregnancies; (2) underperformance on math and reading scores; (3) high prevalence of young people in the juvenile justice system; (4) underperformance on high school graduation rates.

Armed with that information, Durso realized that "the ten poorest zip codes [in New York City] are very fragile with a lack of dads involved in the communities. The kids are living on the system, depending on school lunches. The poverty line is $23,000 per year, which many families fall beneath."

Durso and LEAD.NYC became determined to do something

about it, so they created the 10 Zip Codes Project, in which they would focus on gathering agencies to collaborate in helping the poorest neighborhoods in order to elevate the lives of at-risk youth. The 10 Zip Codes Project finds likeminded church-based or community-based partners with a common passion for the community.

In the project's first phase, Durso and his team chose two communities to create an asset map of agencies working in there. Washington Heights in Upper Manhattan and East New York in Brooklyn with a combined population of 400,000. In Washington Heights, Manhattan Bible Church anchors several partners, including school principals who allow access to four public schools. This access allows LEAD.NYC to create and teach a curriculum called Heart of a Champion, which teaches basic life skills of self-discipline and fostering spiritual disciplines.

The philosophy of the effort recognizes that it is important to meet the holistic needs of people to assist their flourishing including food, education, and mentorship. So they have championed programs such as a feeding program, which Manhattan Bible Church leads. Another partner is Young Life (see chapter 5, Paul Coty), which provides a mentoring program for at-risk African-American men in East New York.

One of the symptoms of at-risk communities is the high prevalence of abortion, due to the economic and family uncertainty that unexpected pregnancies create. Avail is another partner (chapter 6), which provides crisis pregnancy resources. This is a crucial asset in a city with 60,000 abortions a year. One leader commented that because of Planned Parenthood's influence, the African-American community is half its size due to the high number of abortions. As young people from these neighborhoods transition from high school into adulthood, both Columbia University and Nyack College have offered college scholarships to eligible young people. The vision is to care for vulnerable populations from conception into flourishing as adults.

The strategy with the 10 Zip Codes Project is to offer ongoing program offerings with consistent measurement and assessment. The leaders of this project are taking all the lessons learned from ecosystem thinking and applying them to our most fragile neighborhoods. The vision is to see tremendous, measurable impact over the course of a decade.

—————|||—————

A LATIN KING BECOMES A CHILD OF THE KING
The Transformational Impact of
Latino Pastoral Action Center

In 1992 Raymond Rivera began thinking seriously about creating a Latino-led agency in New York City that would provide holistic services to its poorest communities. Rivera had already created an educational program at New York Theological Seminary to provide theological training for Hispanic leaders, but he wanted to help those leaders expand their ministries.

So that year, with an initial grant from a foundation colleague, Rivera launched the Latino Pastoral Action Center (LPAC). LPAC began its work in an office at the New York Missions Society on 21st Street and Park Avenue in Manhattan. And four years later, in 1996, LPAC was ready to formally begin its work. Since then, Rivera has trained and mentored thousands of New York City leaders across the ethnic spectrum.

But by 2012, Rivera, who turned sixty, knew he needed to think about a succession plan for LPAC's leadership. His daughter Susana Rivera Leon was the perfect choice and stepped into her CEO role later that year. "I felt called into ministry at the age of sixteen," she says. "I have always been drawn to the service of others, to the least of these."

Today LPAC's offices are in the Highbridge community of the Bronx, in zip code 10452. This community, explains Leon, is "the poorest congressional district in America. We have the highest numbers of people with social ills—health needs, educational needs, violence, and unemployment. Our immediate fifteen-block community faces a grim picture. At the same time, we have a community filled with culture, promise, and hope."

It's the perfect spot for LPAC's work, which provides a range of community services, including after-school care, a food pantry, internships at LPAC to serve the community, and reentry programs from prison. LPAC's largest program annually assists 2,000 young people aged eighteen to twenty-four with providing an alternative to incarceration. "We offer programming to those who have been charged with misdemeanor to nonviolent felonies who otherwise would be sent to prison," Leon says. "We connect them to programmatic options including Urban Youth Alliance and Bronx Connect."

Another arena of transformative impact has been in birthing charter schools. The first charter school began in 2002 inside of LPAC and became so successful that it was named as one of the top ten schools in New York State. In recognition of LPAC's extraordinary success in educating children in the K-5 grades, New York State asked them to plant more charter schools. Since then, LPAC has birthed three more—two elementary schools and one middle school—and educates 1,500 students a year. A fifth charter school is in planning stages. Given the poverty context of the 10452 zip code, these are remarkable educational achievements.

Through her leadership work with LPAC, Leon has seen firsthand God at work over and over through their efforts and offers three examples. The first one is of Carlos Montes. "I met Carlos Montes in the early 1990s during his Marxist phase at Yale," she says. "We met in youth leadership for advocacy for the poor. Through our friendship he got to see what holistic ministry looked like. My dad told him, 'It is important to see the difference between institutional Christianity and the person of Christ.' The Holy Spirit used that one sentence to cause Montes to accept Jesus. Montes became a director and then a vice president in LPAC. He went to seminary and received a Master of Divinity degree. Now he is the CEO of a nonprofit in New Jersey."

She also tells the story of Mandi Oyola who came to LPAC, which has multiple facilities, wanting to use the gym. She was a local mom, an immigrant from the Dominican Republic who came here to find medical services for her family. She came from a culturally Catholic background. As the result of meeting the LPAC team and encountering the gospel, Oyola accepted the Lord, and now has a personal relationship with Him. "We helped her access college courses through a grant program," Leon says. "She then helped start a daycare center as a full-time volunteer for two years."

Her third story is about Ray Perez, the leader of Latin Kings, a notorious gang, who served more than a decade in prison. He went to jail when he was eighteen. When he came out and got settled into a halfway house, LPAC was his first internship where he worked at their organization on a maintenance team. His time at LPAC drew him to Jesus and he became a believer. Eventually he became the lead supervisor for their work with the recovery population. "He was a Latin King who is now serving the King of kings," she says. "He had a second chance at life. Perez has a restored life with family and children."

God used LPAC to reach a Yale-educated atheist, a Latin King gang leader, and an immigrant mom—among the many thousands of others. Ray Rivera's vision in 1992 has been multiplied in the communities and inspired other similar efforts nationally.

———|||———

THE LAST, THE LEAST, THE LONELY
Ed Morgan Leaves a Successful Career to Champion the Poor

One of the greatest champions for the poor in the past fifty years in New York City has been Ed Morgan. Morgan embodies what it means to have Jesus' heart for the poor and frequently references the 2,000 verses in Scripture regarding God's concerns for them.

In 1986, Morgan was a successful communicator and speechwriter for General Electric's top executives. He had even been the legendary Jack Welch's speechwriter. Even though Morgan's father planted what is now Stone Hill Church in Princeton, Morgan felt as though he had never declared himself as "combatant" for Christ in the Kingdom of Light. Despite being an elder in the church, Morgan decided to get baptized as an adult at the age of forty-seven. His wife, Judy, joined him and was baptized as well.

He never realized what becoming a "combatant for Christ" might look like. "After my baptism all of my problems started," Morgan says. "Within weeks I was no longer liked by the brass at GE. Then I was misdiagnosed with pancreatic cancer. I thought I had a short time to live. I spent two years in fear and not wanting to be at GE."

During this wilderness season, he was introduced to the magazine *Christian Herald* (see chapter 2). It was the parent of The Bowery Mission and from time to time described its impact on the homeless. The *Christian Herald* had been a distinguished American coffee-table magazine for 100 years and was now floundering. Morgan knew the communications world and was inspired to help.

In 1992, after several years of volunteering his time and services, Morgan joined the *Christian Herald*/The Bowery staff as CEO with a full-time salary of $40,000. Though it was a far cry from what he had made at GE, he took it, since he felt as though he had done nothing significant with his life—and this was his opportunity to change that. His second son had just entered Vanderbilt and had steep tuition costs. Yet Morgan said yes to the offer. Miraculously, his son Chris received a full scholarship through the United States Navy that very fall.

Morgan stepped into his role, and over the next twenty-two years, he led the organization from the verge of insolvency to becoming one of the most robust rescue missions in America. When Morgan left The Bowery in 2015, the ministry had grown dramatically. More importantly, it had seen more than 1,100 lives radically transformed and had a healthy balance sheet. God breathed on Morgan's vision and skills to radically transform The Bowery.

Morgan says his guiding vision all those years was to "reach the last, the least, and the lonely of New York City and see their lives transformed." The Bowery, he explains, focuses on serving New York's street people. "After the city houses 60,000 in the shelter system, there are another 3,800 homeless who have no place to sleep. Among homeless men, more than 90 percent are raised fatherless. Boys need someone to look up to and to provide loving correction. Young men grow up with street values. We want to change that."

Morgan has been singularly successful in casting vision for the poor to the investor community, most of whom are not giving from a faith motivation. "There were not enough Christians living in the city to resource a growing Bowery," he says. "I wanted to appeal to both Christian and humanitarian donors. We promoted measurable changes toward transformed lives. We were able to transform the 'Gala art form' into a Christian engine for financial support."

Today, The Bowery provides shelter every night for more than 150 people while providing more than 400,000 meals a year. Programming reflects the tripartite nature of every person—body, soul, and spirit. The Bowery also provides skill training for its residents to become self-sufficient upon graduation.

Morgan shares the story of James Macklin as an example. In 1988, Macklin was sleeping on a subway and awakened by a woman who sent him to The Bowery. He came into the program and graduated in 1989. He had been so transformed that after his graduation, Morgan asked him to become the associate director of The Bowery, because of the men's respect for him. He later became a primary ambassador for The Bowery.

Morgan is now president emeritus and continues his work coaching for some of the 300 other rescue missions throughout the country. He has a profound understanding of the challenges facing the church in its need to embrace the least, the lost, and the lonely. The vision is to multiply the effectiveness of The Bowery Mission into other cities—inspiring leadership to draw the most vulnerable into the welcoming arms of Jesus through the church.

LIFE ON LIFE
Danny Sanabria Leads Youth for Christ into Juvenile Centers

At the age of sixteen, Danny Sanabria was an angry young man. He was the son of Puerto Rican immigrants living in Brooklyn. "I hated church. I hated everyone," Sanabria says. "Then I was radically converted and wanted to share this newfound love with everyone." Something he has been passionately doing for a decade now.

In 2009, Sanabria launched a prayer walk for young people, which he called, "God Belongs in My City." The prayer walk started at multiple locations throughout the city and culminated after an hour of walking to Times Square in Midtown Manhattan. For the first six years, 1,000 young people participated, finding out about the prayer walk from alumni and through social media. Dressed in GOD BELONGS IN MY CITY T-shirts, the young people arrived at their designated time in Times Square and then collectively knelt to pray for God to move powerfully in the city. The prayer walk became so successful and gained so much attention that faith organizations throughout the world took Sanabria's model and adopted it. Today those prayer walks occur in eighty cities globally.

In the past five years, Sanabria's leadership assignment has shifted from primarily leading God Belongs in My City to impact young people through Youth for Christ in New York City's juvenile justice system. "We have 2,500 young people in the juvenile justice system in New York City," Sanabria explains. "We work with every single young person in the facilities where we are present. We have public readings of Scripture in the hallways using audio Scripture. We have found it to be very impactful for troubled young people to hear the Good News of the gospel. The guards even ask questions about God. We are the only program coming into the facilities because young people wanted a church presence."

Sanabria said that the critical success factor in their work is by mobilizing mentors to interact with young people. "Currently 99 percent of the young people being mentored come from our poorest zip codes. Our vision is to enlist 1,000 mentors who will interact with 10,000 young people in the facilities and continue with them upon their departure. It really comes down to life-on-life discipleship."

Sanabria believes this kind of mentoring is something the churches can get involved with, that they can provide an army of mentors who invest time, money, and connection to a larger family to give these young people a future.

Mentors to the poor matter. "Lynn Marie was mentoring a young homeless girl," Sanabria says. "She became her family. Lynn Marie went to the facility every week for two years and mentored the girl. When the young girl got out of the facility, Lynn Marie was committed to her basic needs. That meant providing a place to stay on occasion, food to eat, and even letting her use Lynn Marie's shower. Meeting basic needs can be transformative for those without access to anything."

The work that YFC does is preventative. Sanabria's brother, John, who is a captain with the New York police department, gave Sanabria a book of some of the criminals in New York City. Sanabria saw that the ages on their rap sheets of when their lives of crime started were fourteen, fifteen, seventeen. John told him, "If you reach them young, I won't have to arrest them later."

Sanabria has made a tremendous difference in the city by galvanizing young people of faith to demonstrate their unity in New York City. His impact is now being multiplied as he mobilizes adults into a movement of investing in our most vulnerable young people. It is in the cells and hallways of juvenile centers where young people discover not only that God belongs in the city but in the center of their lives.

———— ||| ————

AN URBAN VILLAGE IN EAST NEW YORK
A. R. Bernard and Jamaal Bernard Lead
an Historic Housing Initiative

Engaging the poor and economically challenged is a complex undertaking. There are layers of factors that culminate in the flourishing of a community or to its becoming disadvantaged. Critical to these factors is affordable housing.

A. R. Bernard and his son, Jamaal, pastor the Christian Cultural Center (CCC), with the mother campus in East New York. CCC has become the largest church in New York City and on the East Coast, with a weekly average on-site attendance of 10,000 and total membership of 43,000. A. R. Bernard is a once-in-a-century leader who navigates the sacred and civic spaces of New York City with ease and extraordinary effectiveness. (He is also an enormous champion for the work of Movement Day and LEAD.NYC. Bernard has spoken for us in New York City on many occasions, as well as at the birthing of Movement Day Dubai in March 2019.)

Jamaal Bernard is a contemporary and best friend of Adam Durso (see "10 Zip Codes Project"). Their friendship embodies the camaraderie of a generation of leaders in New York City who have journeyed together for twenty years even, as they are in their early forties. Jamaal works closely with his father as he leads CCC's Long Island campus. Jamaal has also been instrumental in planting daughter campuses in Orlando.

But both Bernards understand that to affect change for the gospel, we need to go into the community and be on the front edge of helping to meet the needs of the marginalized—including housing. So they created a vision for a decadal housing initiative that will provide housing for 2,100 families in their East New York, Brooklyn community. A. R. also created drawings of what the $1.2 billion project would look like. I believe it is the largest community-development project in American church history.

A. R. shared the vision with me, Ray Bakke, and a number of international doctoral of ministry students. At the end of Bernard's presentation, Bakke summarized what I believe we were all thinking: "Every mayor in America would want to see this presentation."

Speaking to the vision behind the urban village, Jamaal says, "Historically, our society has warehoused the poor into large housing projects. We recognize the needs in a community for it to be sustainable—community spaces, gathering spaces for entertainment, access to affordable retail outlets, access to affordable food, all within walking distances. We believe that a mixed-income housing model is far more sustainable."

And yet one of the great challenges in New York City is affordable housing. A sister city to New York with similar challenges is Hong Kong. At Movement Day Hong Kong in March 2018, Andrew Gardner said that New York City and Hong Kong face the greatest housing challenges of any two cities in the world. The housing project is being done in collaboration with Gotham Development. It is a partnership model that is applicable to any major city in the world. The housing challenges facing cities will require innovative solutions.

Jamaal describes their neighborhood as a large population of civil servants who are being priced out of the housing market due to gentrification. "We want people who have lived in these neighborhoods their entire lives to be able to stay without being forced out," he says.

The vision is that, in addition to meeting community needs, next-generation leaders in other cities will multiply this model. Jamaal sees these next few years as critical to the health of Christianity in New York City and other US cities. "I see God raising up many younger leaders who are participating in the succession of leaders in our churches," he says. "We are also seeing the opportunity to reproduce an impactful, sustainable model in cities. We are planting CCC campuses not only in Orlando but in other East Coast cities that will be connected to the Brooklyn campus. This aligns with my calling to be a shepherd to attract people to Jesus."

The CCC and Urban Village model are enormous signs of hope for East New York and the cities of the globe. Effective succession planning and innovative models are creating an opportunity to better the lives of tens of thousands of urban dwellers by 2030.

———|||———

IMAGO DEI
Chris Whitford Leads Avail on Behalf of Families in New York City

At the core of wanting to impact millions of people for the gospel is the recognition of the *Imago Dei* in every person—the image of God. Chris Whitford and her team embody this in extraordinary ways through the impact of Avail in New York City.

On December 5, 2019, Whitford led the devotional at our monthly prayer gathering in Manhattan. She is the CEO of Avail NYC, an organization committed to working with those facing unexpected pregnancies. I was struck by how she described the gospel: "The gospel levels the audience before the wonder and awe of grace." Whitford clearly has a gift of getting people of faith to see the world differently, in a way that draws attention to God's redemptive activity.

Leading an organization like Avail in New York City is a daunting challenge. According to Whitford, 60,000 abortions occur in New York City every year. Nationally one in four American women have had an abortion by the age of forty. In New York City, 30 percent of pregnancies end in abortion.

"The biggest challenge is that abortion and unexpected pregnancies are understood only in political terms," Whitford says. "Our posture is to see people in the ways God sees them, the *Imago Dei*, the image of God in everyone. We don't use our Christian faith to politicize what people are experiencing with an unexpected pregnancy."

Whitford says that in their work, four people are included in every conversation—the client, the advocate, the child, and the Lord. God does the persuading on what the next best decision is for the person or couple seeking support.

Avail offers four programmatic expressions to the 1,000 clients they interact with every year:

- **Avail Empower:** for those who think abortion is their only option. They empower the client to imagine a future where they and their child thrive.
- **Avail Equip:** to help clients parent with confidence. They have a network of 200 social agencies to meet the practical needs of the parents. In one of those resources, Avail provides qualifying clients with subsidized childcare for three years.
- **Avail Hope:** a healing program for those who have experienced abortion. They want to help couples experience resiliency amid their unresolved feelings.
- **Avail Flourish:** a healthy-relationships program for couples who need support navigating their network of interpersonal relationships, especially within the context of an unexpected pregnancy or abortion experience.

Whitford loves seeing the transformation that happens with Avail's clients. "We received an email from a client who decided to carry her baby to term," she says. "She described the hardship but then said, 'Who would have guessed that my son is the best part of my life, the easiest part of my life?'"

Whitford's vision for the church is to see it become the leading institution in the response to human need. She longs for a day when the local church becomes the first place rather than the last place that women and couples turn when facing the complexity of an abortion decision. "We want the church to become grace saturated in how we think about unexpected pregnancies," she says. "Jesus was full of grace and love for every person He met. Consider Zacchaeus, the woman at the well, the woman caught in adultery. We want to see the removal of shame from this enormous challenge." Avail reminds the church that if we want to successfully share the gospel and see the landscape of Christianity thrive by 2030, we must see the *Imago Dei* in every person and value every life.

Chapter 7

MARKETPLACE

In October 2010, one month after the inaugural Movement Day gathering, I met Bob Doll in Cape Town, South Africa. We were both attending the Third Lausanne Congress, a network of faith leaders (which began in 1974 under the leadership of Billy Graham and John Stott) across the globe who seek to connect ideas and leaders to advance the gospel. Tim Keller was also there as a keynote speaker on the theme of cities. I was attending as a delegate.

One morning Tim Keller and I invited Bob Doll to breakfast to introduce him to The New York City Movement Project (see chapter 1) and enlist him to join our efforts. Keller and I believed that having an influential marketplace leader was essential for the project to get off the ground.

Why Doll?

Doll was a lead investor in the Lausanne Congress at Cape Town. Prior to the conference, Doug Birdsall, Lausanne's executive director, arranged a meeting with the Dolls to discuss their participation. Doll had in mind to make a $100,000 investment in Lausanne. Birdsall challenged him and Leslie to add a zero to their thinking. The Dolls agreed and invested $1 million in the Cape Town congress. (The fruit of that investment allowed for the Lausanne Movement to be completely revitalized.) Doll had demonstrated a receptivity to invest in big ideas that would catalyze enormous Kingdom impact, which got our attention.

After Doll's Cape Town meeting with Keller and me, both he and Leslie agreed to join us in The New York City Movement Project. We had a follow-up meeting on February 14, 2011, at the Redeemer offices with Keller, Bob and Leslie Doll, me, and Lloyd Reeb from Half Time, an organization that provides coaching for senior marketplace leaders to envision the impact of the last decades of their lives. We felt that Half Time expertise would assist those marketplace leaders in their own spiritual journey even as those same leaders assisted us. As we presented our vision, everyone quickly got on board and we determined that we would each have distinct roles in the project.

My team would convene leaders to participate in the project, Keller and Redeemer provided training, and the Dolls and Reeb would invite marketplace peers to participate. The Dolls would also participate in Half Time over the course of a year. We watched in awe as God used the Half Time cohort to enlist other marketplace leaders to join the project as well. Since that meeting and the results that followed, we have seen the power of an alliance between marketplace leaders, pastors, and mission-agency leaders to reach people for the gospel.

In the past decade since that first meeting, Doll has become a huge influence in the city gospel movement and has influenced hundreds of other marketplace leaders to participate in Movement Day Expressions in their own cities. Doll has also served as a regular speaker at several Movement Day gatherings globally. (See "100X" later in this chapter.) His involvement has also inspired marketplace leaders to seriously consider the role of their faith and vocation in their own context.

Marketplace leaders play a unique role in influencing their own cities for the gospel. They bring three enormous strengths to the city gospel movement conversation: (1) they have cultural influence far beyond pastors and nonprofit leaders; (2) they have strategic acumen developed from building their own businesses/professions; (3) they have philanthropic capacity. As we look toward 2030, marketplace leader involvement is critical to our success. Their engagement will influence churches, agencies, and civic leaders to come to the table.

Marketplace Leaders Are Multipliers

Along with Bob Doll, other strategic marketplace leaders who got involved with The New York City Movement Project were Raymond and Marydel Harris (Dallas), D. G. and Gini Elmore (Bloomington, Illinois), and Ray and Denise Nixon (Dallas). These four couples have provided their strategic acumen, hospitality, introductions to networks, and generosity, and have traveled the globe with our growing Movement Day family. What began as an idea in New York is now present in 200 cities. Committed Christian marketplace leaders are multipliers.

The first continent outside North America to adopt the Movement Day model was Africa. The marketplace leaders there who opened the door were Darin and Paula Owen. Darin is an entrepreneur involved in ten companies. He has Jewish roots and made a faith commitment as a young marketplace leader. Paula oversees an orphanage in their Durban, South Africa, community.

I met the Owens at the Christian Economic Forum through the invitation of Raymond Harris. When Darin heard about Movement Day, he came to see the model in New York that October 2013. He was so impressed that he then brought his Durban colleagues to see the model in 2014. They in turn created an organization called City Story to manage the many initiatives in their own city.

In 2016, Durban, South Africa, represented more than 100 leaders to Movement Day Global Cities. The Durban cohort represented the largest number of leaders from one city outside the United States. And it all began with the influence and initiative of Darin and Paula Owen—marketplace leaders.

One of the early definitions of a city gospel movement was that it is a movement taking place when the Christian population is growing faster than the general population, when there is measurable progress against social ills (such as homelessness and trafficking), and when Christian leaders are finding their way into places of cultural influence. Looking particularly at cultural influence, in 2008, Tim Keller reflected that marketplace leaders had three arenas of cultural influence: knowledge (research university, think tanks), aesthetics (literature, theater, dance), and morals (law schools). He also reflected that there were three degrees of influence, simply noted as A, B, and C, with A being the highest level and C being the lowest. Keller's assessment was that the Christian community in New York had achieved only a level C in influence.[1]

In the past twelve years, the faith and work movements have taken strategic strides to address these gaps. For instance, they have birthed different incubator fellowships with a long-term view of landing serious Christian leaders in the cockpit of their professions. Gotham Fellowship is an example of this type of initiative. Redeemer Presbyterian Church created "an intensive, top-tier program to equip participants for gospel leadership in New York City and the world."[2] As a nine-month program, Gotham Fellowship takes its participants through theological training, spiritual and personal development, and community formation.

A parallel movement is Christian Union New York City. Christian Union seeks to network their alumni from their campus work, along with their peers, who are living in New York City. Their purpose is to "create robust, interconnected networks that engage their fields and community with the Gospel in ways that nourish goodness, truth, justice, and beauty."[3] They achieve this connectedness through a strong emphasis on corporate prayer, fasting, salons (gatherings with thought leaders), and conferences.

For gospel impact in a city to take place, there needs to be a robust pipeline of leadership built from university into the marketplace. The pipeline has historically not been as robust as is necessary to influence New York City. Bob Doll has estimated that earlier in his career, he was often the only identifiable Christian in many of his workplace settings.

Josh Crossman picks up this theme in *The Great Opportunity* when he discusses long-term witness. He is specifically thinking about the university setting, but it stands to reason that if it is true of the university, and they are graduating professionals into the marketplace, the info applies to the marketplace as well. Crossman writes, "Our research indicates that in the mainstream academy, among traditionally ranked top 40 institutions, Christians comprise less than 3 percent of the professionals, and in the humanities, less than 2 percent."[4]

There are signs of hope in the university setting, however,

with the growth of campus efforts like InterVarsity, which is quadrupling the number of area teams in New York City from one to four for the first time in its almost eighty-year history. InterVarsity has also had a rapidly growing graduate student fellowship movement across the United States. Historic movements like InterVarsity, The Navigators, Cru, and Christian Union are extraordinarily important members of this ecosystem.

The Every Campus movement has a vision to plant a chapter on every US campus. There are currently more than eighty partner agencies. This is a powerful ecosystem of leaders who have a shared vision for the future. And just as important, this is the pipeline for future marketplace-leader Christians to address the gaps currently experienced in the New York City and national landscape. This pipeline of leaders represents the current and future leadership of the church toward the 2030 vision.[5]

What Needs to Happen

Manhattan is the epicenter of marketplace activity. During the workweek, Manhattan's population explodes to 4 million people, including 1.63 million commuters.[6] Commuting is an important aspect of consideration when we aim to reach those in the marketplace. With the intense commuter culture, most New Yorkers struggle with "time poverty," in which people are challenged by their obligations to working and commuting.

Given the challenges of time constraints for marketplace leaders, we must give serious consideration to the most strategic arenas of engagement. We have outlined several of those arenas in chapters 4–6: planting new churches, investing in the next generation, and engaging the poor. We believe that by aggregating time, talent, and treasure around specific initiatives we can see an extraordinary acceleration of those initiatives.

Craig Sider, CEO of Movement.org; Chip Roper, president and founder of the VOCA Center (VOCA is short for vocation); and Scott Crosby of Christian Union represented the marketplace working group to address the question of how a community of Manhattan marketplace Christians can scale the great work already happening. Together they have interacted with many of the leading Christian marketplace leaders across Metro New York City in order to discern the most strategic way forward.

According to Roper, to increase the influence of Christian marketplace leaders in Manhattan, which he estimates to be 60,000, it is essential for them to join a faith and work group. He believes that by doing so, it will continue to increase the density of the network of Christian professionals in New York City. They can connect with one another, mature in their faith, and support and encourage one another in sharing the gospel in the marketplace.

Sider has proposed the formation of a 100-member cohort of 50 percent marketplace leader and 50 percent pastoral leadership by 2021. The thought behind this model is that influential leaders who span the ecosystem of both church and marketplace can address issues together that they cannot do without one another. A cohort that could be launched and meet perhaps twice a year could give oversight to very strategic citywide initiatives.

Given the cultural differences between Manhattan and the outer boroughs and suburbs, this cohort could bring together remarkably diverse leaders. That diversity would be geographic, vocational, and cultural. An historical model is the Clapham sect from nineteenth-century England, which William Wilberforce, the great Parliamentarian, led, and which also included a banker, a brewer, a writer, and several pastors. Wilberforce's vision was to end slavery and to amend child labor laws. The spiritual force of the Clapham sect, with the deep commitment to pray three times a day as well engage in strategic legislation, ended slavery in the United Kingdom.

Imagine the possibilities if marketplace leaders and pastoral leaders in New York City were to agree on the top three challenges facing the city. Having common language and common outcomes over the course of a decade could be game-changing.

This common language could be fused into all the existing and multiplying marketplace groups across the city. The principles of educating, aggregating, and coordinating efforts could be enormously powerful. Imagine the future if a broad community of marketplace leaders were engaged to fully assist Young Life in reaching its goal of impacting 100,000 young people by 2026. Consider what could happen if marketplace leaders were taught the principles of providing affordable housing from the Christian Cultural Center and then trained their peers nationally? Imagine marketplace leaders bringing their professional peers in larger numbers to assist the many emerging church plants across the region. Envision 60,000 marketplace leaders praying for their peers to gain the most influential positions in the arenas of university board rooms, law schools, and political offices.

We believe it can be more than imagination. We believe this can be reality.

Possibilities

To see the full impact of faith in the marketplace and from the marketplace to the rest of the city, we need to be strategic. I recommend the following:

- Marketplace Christians can identify workplace fellowship groups in their own city to participate in. If none exist, start a chapter. Contacts in this chapter can connect you to efforts like the New Canaan Society and employee groups like those at American Express.
- Read the best literature available on this topic, including *Every Good Endeavor* by Tim Keller, *Half Time* by Bob Buford, and *The Call* by Os Guinness. A roster of ten recommended books are provided on the Institute for Faith, Work, and Economics website (tifwe.org).
- Identify and invest in a next-generation leader in your sphere of expertise. Opportunities are available through connections to university organizations (InterVarsity, Cru, The Navigators, Christian Union).
- Create a life plan by participating in Half Time or through a coaching experience. This will give you time to interpret where God is leading you for the coming two to four decades of your life.
- Join a citywide effort to address an enormous need (church planting, engaging the poor, discipling the next generation). Bring others along with you.
- Assist in the formation of a citywide cohort of marketplace leaders and pastors to build friendship, become fluent in your city's greatest challenges, and agree on a decadal plan of action.

History has taught us that a small group of committed marketplace Christian leaders can change the fulcrum of history. There is no better place and no better time than right now in New York City to see this come to fruition.

100X
Bob Doll Leverages His Global Marketplace Platform for the Gospel

God is using the cultural influence, strategic acumen, and philanthropic generosity as described in this chapter by strategic marketplace leaders. One of those leaders is Bob Doll and his wife, Leslie.

Bob and Leslie Doll joined the Half Time cohort in the spring of 2011. Half Time exists to help leaders in understanding their calling and to maximize their impact for the remainder of their lives. Bob Buford, Half Time's founder, describes it as giving leaders a vision to increase their impact by 100X.

In 2012, Doll lost his position at BlackRock as their chief equity strategist. It was a devastating turn of events for him. "I realized that the center of my identity had become my work," he says, reflecting on that time in his life. "Half Time came at just the right moment to help me determine what the core of my calling was."

At the end of that Half Time experience, Doll drafted a personal mission statement: "I will with God's help, maintain and enhance a global platform and voice through my ability to manage money and speak about financial markets, so that I can use both money and a Christian worldview to impact and serve organizations and Christian business groups at the convergence of faith and work so as to enable ministry and increase commitment to Christian faith in life and work."

As of 2020, Doll is fulfilling his mission statement in extraordinary ways. He is currently the chief equity strategist at Nuveen Financial. His weekly newsletter is read by more than 225,000 subscribers. He appears fifty times a year on television to discuss the markets on CNBC, Fox Business, and Bloomberg. His annual ten predictions are carried in the *Wall Street Journal*. Doll may be the most visible Christian on Wall Street.

In his Christian leadership Doll works on ten boards, including Lausanne, Kingdom Advisors, National Christian Foundation, Word of Life, and as board chair of Movement.org.

Leslie Doll channels her energy to impact the Middle East by working closely with Strategic Resource Group, an agency to impact the Middle East with the gospel. She has a burden for the forgotten Christian women living in unstable Middle Eastern countries. She has traveled within 200 miles of ISIS camps to encourage these vulnerable communities.

Both Bob and Leslie Doll have been extraordinary voices for Movement Day globally. They began attending in 2011 in New York City. Bob has been to every New York City gathering since then. The Dolls have both spoken for Movement Day in London, Dubai, and several US cities.

Doll sees his assignment as to "impact his peers in the industry—whether they be apathetic, agnostic, or spiritually engaged."

Doll is excited to see what is working in the faith and work movement. "The movement is making great progress," he says. "Ten years ago, there were very few people who were aware.

Now most people in the church have heard about it. I spoke at a Denver Institute for Faith and Work and 500 attended. At the Lausanne Congress on Work Forum in Manila in 2019, about half the attendees were deeply engaged and half were getting engaged."

When he thinks about being involved with organizations that increase their impact, he mentions his work with Movement.org. "Movement.org is a 100X initiative that brings together marketplace leaders, pastors, and nonprofit leaders to scale impact in their cities," he says. "I have never seen anything like it in my lifetime."

Bob and Leslie Doll represent the possibilities of how God can use surrendered lives of those at the peak of their careers and influence. Their journey speaks to the power of discovery in a person's life calling and then acting on it. The global Christian movement has been deeply enriched by their influence.

———— ||| ————

FRIENDSHIP IN JESUS
Tom Cole Leads the New Canaan Society Movement in New York City

An enduring gospel movement will require a growing community of leaders with a deepening sense of friendship. Tom Cole has been a great voice for the value of friendship among marketplace leaders in Manhattan.

Cole is the managing director and co-head of Leveraged Finance at Citibank. He arrived in New York from Chicago. Cole had been part of a church men's group that had been highly effective, but he could not find one in New York.

"Before moving to New York, I went through a personal crisis in my divorce," he says. "I had been surrounded by men who breathed truth into me. I was eager to see that kind of group in New York. I met Eric Metaxas, the author, who said we could start something."

The group they had in mind was the New Canaan Society (NCS), a movement Jim Lane founded in 1995. Lane had a significant career on Wall Street and saw the need for male friendship to thrive in an extraordinarily intense environment. So Lane, Cole, and friends created NCS as a gathering of men who get together regularly to be challenged in their faith walk and to discover friendship in Jesus with one another, and who they encourage to join small groups on the off weeks. NCS had its first meetings in Lane's living room in New Canaan, Connecticut. The group soon mushroomed to more than 200 men hungry for friendship who would arrive on a Friday morning trying to find parking in Lane's neighborhood.

NCS was exactly what Cole was looking for, and in 2005, he founded a chapter in Manhattan, which meets every other Thursday during the school year. It became so successful, Cole later ran the national NCS for two years.

Today there are a dozen NCS chapters in Metro New York and sixty nationally, along with international interest in London. "We are all about friendship in Jesus and friendship with others," Cole says. "NCS is the gasoline that fosters this friendship as guys attend and engage one another."

In the context of their gatherings, Cole has noticed the sheer number of broken families that the men represent. "Nothing gets a man to weep like talking about his father," he says. "We have a strong emphasis on both Mother's Day and Father's Day. We really want men to reconnect with their families."

Cole sees the fruit of the NCS discipleship model as giving men confidence to be bold in their faith in the workplace. He believes that as men are rooted in friendship, they will be more secure to talk openly about their faith in an often hostile work environment.

NCS is also a way of helping their members express love and generosity in the workplace. "The biggest Google search is, 'Why are Christians so negative and judgmental?' Our vision is for our members to be countercultural to that perception in their Christlikeness. I want our members to be perceived as normal, those who love their neighbors."

Cole reflects on one story that particularly affected him: "We had a member who had never heard 'I love you' from his father. We challenged our members to write our fathers. This member wrote his dad, and they decided to meet in Central Park for a one-on-one meeting. They met and it was an extraordinarily healing time for him."

As men in the marketplace become more human, Cole believes their witness will become more attractive to others. His vision is to see men have a greater confidence in talking about their faith in the context of Manhattan workplaces. He believes that men sharing their faith and engaged in vibrant friendship will change the culture of a city, which will in turn change the world.

MARKETPLACE LEADERS FLOURISHING
Chip Roper Plants the VOCA Center in New York City

A gospel ecosystem of marketplace Christians in any city is vital. In New York City, it is a prerequisite for a gospel movement to flourish. New York City is vocationally centric as people travel from around the world to come to New York to work. Chip Roper has been growing the ecosystem through his leadership with the VOCA Center.

When Roper graduated high school, his ambition was to make as much money as possible. He viewed the business world as a vehicle to pursue wealth, not create value. He then realized he did not know how to run his own life, let alone a business.

He experienced a dramatic turnaround in his early twenties. He saw the need to surrender his life to Christ and, after college, went to seminary after college at Trinity University outside of Chicago. He was shaped by the Willow Creek movement and got involved there for three years, where he was influenced by the "pro-business" message of Willow Creek and Bill Hybels. Even after entering the pastorate, his favorite days were getting out of the office to visit his parishioners in their work environments.

During his first fifteen years in the pastoral ministry, he

never heard anyone talk about theology of vocation. His elders encouraged him to learn as much as he could about this "common grace" of faith and work. In 2014, Roper made the bold decision to leave the pastorate and move to New York City to start the VOCA Center. "I did a listening tour in 2015 and discovered my lane—helping people discern their vocational path," he says.

In the past five years, Roper has emerged as an extraordinary subject matter expert and friend to senior marketplace leaders in the Manhattan Christian community. He regularly emcees the New Canaan Society.

Roper's assignment is a crucial one, given the global significance of Manhattan-based professionals. Through the VOCA Center, Roper provides personal coaching, seminars with industry leaders, and blogs that inform the thinking of faith marketplace leaders globally.

He views his calling as providing incarnational ministry to business leaders through discipleship, evangelism, and connecting business leaders to Kingdom opportunities. His model includes a donor-based and a fee-based side for VOCA. "I wanted my clients to see that I understand their world, having to hustle for business just like they do."

As he considers what's working with marketplace Christian leaders, he says, "I am privileged to expose Christian marketplace role models to their peers, leaders like Bob Doll and Cheryl Batchelder, who served as CEO of Pier 1 Imports and AFC Enterprises. Business networks are flourishing. Generosity NYC encourages strategic philanthropy and is part of the national generosity movement. New Canaan Society is also a national network with several Metro NYC chapters."

Roper's decadal vision is to see 50 percent of the 60,000

marketplace Christians in Manhattan in a vocationally based group that affirms their calling as marketplace Christians. "This would validate their calling and connect them to other believers," he says. Roper's vision is important to the flourishing of individuals as well as to the flourishing of the city spiritually. As this vision comes to fruition, it will make an extraordinary contribution to the rapidly growing ecosystem of Christian marketplace leaders in New York City, who in turn will impact the globe together.

Chapter 8

2030

I n April 1987, Rick Richardson, an InterVarsity area director in Illinois, convened 1,000 people from diverse church and ethnic backgrounds to pray together on a Friday night at Moody Church in Chicago. Baptists and Pentecostals, Methodists and Lutherans, African Americans, Hispanics, Asians, and Anglos came together for a powerful time of prayer and fellowship.

We can do that in New York City, I thought when I heard about that gathering.

So that June I met with Ted Gandy and Aida Force of Here's Life Inner City (HLIC), the urban ministry arm of Campus Crusade. They had developed a network of 600 churches in New York City from the "I Found It" campaign of the 1970s. We met in their 44th Street offices in Manhattan. As I laid out my desire for a similar prayer gathering for NYC, they quickly came on board, and we decided to convene sixteen churches to pray together on February 5, 1988, at First Baptist Church of Flushing, my home church.

HLIC's responsibility was to promote the gathering, get sixteen photographs of participating pastors, and circulate the advertisement. My responsibility was to shape the program with David Bryant, the founder of Concerts of Prayer International (see chapter 9), and to get the facility ready.

On February 5, we did not have sixteen churches participate. We had seventy-five.

At that moment, I learned two things: there is power when we unite and agree together in prayer,[1] and we build a multiplier effect by having a backbone organization or backbone alliance lead the charge to facilitate the efforts of everyone in the ecosystem.[2] If we have agreement and intelligent coordination, we see God create exponential results.

The 2030 Vision and a Backbone Organization

In the thirty years following the first Concerts of Prayer gathering, 2,000 churches have been knit together in diverse prayer gatherings. That praying led us to do mission together—whether in planting churches, assisting the poor, or influencing the next generation. Over the past year, our Co-Lab team has convened four working groups and more than eighty stakeholders to craft a vision for 2030 to see God engage hundreds of thousands of people over the coming decade, and to foster broad agreement across churches, mission agencies, marketplace leaders, and community groups to help make it happen—as there is great power in agreement and unity.

As we look at implementing that vision, we recognize that centrally critical to making it a reality is for us to have a strong backbone organization working with an alliance of ecosystem partners. The role of this backbone organization is to:

- Create a common agenda. In our case we have used the principles from *The Great Opportunity* as an organizing document to help us focus on our common vision and strategy.
- Share our measurement. We can plan and strategize, but without the ability to measure our success, we have no way to know if our plans are on the right course. To that end, the backbone organization directs our engagement with a research partner and creates a dashboard with quarterly updates.
- Create mutuality. We report on the progress of the plan as we convene leaders in our large gatherings three times a year. From year to year, we need to evaluate the measurement, report on our work, and build or adjust our work. The backbone organization will lead us through that annual review by using the historical platforms of the Pastor's Prayer Summit (thirty years), Global Leadership Summit (fifteen years), and Movement Day (ten years) where a critical mass of leaders gather annually.
- Oversee continuous communications: the backbone organization will create or oversee monthly communications from the ecosystem and to the ecosystem to reinforce developments and updates, and to encourage and motivate us in our endeavors.
- Provide backbone support. The backbone organization provides reports and next steps to keep ecosystem agencies abreast of the plan's status and how we can proceed or reevaluate.
- Secure funding for strategic initiatives and agencies.[3]

As we have considered all that a strong backbone organization needs to be and who might be the right leader in that capacity, it became obvious that LEAD.NYC under the direction of Adam Durso will give oversight to the 2030 vision. Durso has shown enormously capable leadership, given his longevity of twenty-five years of work in New York City alongside strong relationships with the mayor's office, New York State leadership, and as a liaison with the White House on behalf of New York City faith leaders. Mark Matlock of WisdomWorks is also a central facilitator as we develop our plans. Matlock has thirty years of experience and a working partnership with the research team at the Barna Group.

Under their guidance and support, we feel we are in the best position to see 2030 become a reality.

The Plan: A Starting Point for Impacting 1 Million People in Metro NYC by 2030

Obviously reaching 1 million people in Metro NYC for the gospel within the next decade is a huge undertaking—one we realize requires hearing wisdom and discernment from multiple voices. So we have interviewed twenty-two leaders and have worked with eighty stakeholders or agencies with whom we have the most history, listening, taking notes, praying, filtering, and uniting on important points about the nature of our vision and plan. This is what we have learned so far:

First, this is just a starting point. We want this to be an organic process that involves an ever-increasing number of leaders to add to the plan with their efforts, which point toward cumulative impact. Though we started with this smaller group, our strategy is to widen the circle of participants to better shape a larger plan in our Movement Day methodology. We have asked Mark Matlock, our facilitative expert from

WisdomWorks, to give us his insight and leadership on this widening strategy.

Second, we recognize that we are only a small slice of what God is doing in Metro New York City. We represent an important slice, but only a slice. In humility we offer before God our best understanding and thinking.

Third, we fully expect to encounter a lot of surprises along the way. God is working in so many powerful ways that we cannot even imagine. This will require the intentionality of unity and the discipline of story gathering and storytelling. New York City is like an onion that one needs to continue to peel off dozens of layers.

The Plan's Methodology

Armed with information and wisdom from our numerous interviews and meetings, we have put together a four-fold methodology to move us on a path toward measurable success:

Education: We begin by familiarizing ourselves with the context of our vision and strategy. We did this in chapters 2 and 3, along with snapshots of leaders in action, which we included in chapters 4 through 7.

Incubation: There are efforts that need to be birthed because they do not currently exist. Like the 1988 Concerts of Prayer story, we are bringing together agencies to work together in new and multiplicative ways.

Advocacy: Several mature organizations are already doing spectacular work—Young Life, Thrive Collective, The Bowery Mission, City to City, as well as many others. The role of the plan is to promote their work and enlist participants and investors to help scale their work. We do not need to reinvent the wheel.

Communication: LEAD.NYC will use its monthly, quarterly, and annual platforms to message the progress on the plan. We will use the emerging dashboard as a web-based resource for leaders to get updates on our collective progress. We will invite all the participating stakeholders to communicate 2030's progress with their constituents. This book will serve as an important reference point for 2030's launch and continuation. Our hope is that this book will catalyze dozens of city teams to write similar essays and books for their own context. The more we know about our past collectively, the more we will care about our future. A new element will be a dashboard that the group will create and update quarterly to report on the plan's progress.

While we want to start at "home" by influencing and changing Metro New York City's landscape for the gospel, our overall vision is to mobilize other cities—both domestic and international—to have a ten-year vision and a twelve-month rhythm as well.

Five Plan Elements We Can Incorporate

Every plan needs a roadmap and a rhythm. The elements of these plans have emerged after a year of working group conversations and from thirty-five years of reflection on best practices.

Element #1: Daily, Quarterly, and Annual Prayer for 2030's Outcomes

- Each month our current 300 Pastor's Prayer Summit alumni will receive a monthly prayer guide that captures the themes and updates of the 2030 plan.
- Church of the City has agreed to use the recommendations from *The Great Opportunity* in its daily and on-going prayer efforts. This will serve as a model for

other churches to adopt. LEAD.NYC will invite 200 churches to join this prayer effort in its gatherings throughout the year.

- Christian Union will be invited to take each month's prayer guide and invite leaders to fast and pray two times a year for forty days in its ongoing campaigns.
- Pray.nyc will highlight the prayer guide themes in their quarterly gatherings with 5,000 leaders each. In its first three virtual meetings in 2020, attendance has been 43,000 participants.
- LEAD.NYC will lead the January Pastor's Prayer Summit and May National Day of Prayer efforts for 250 Metro leaders and their churches.
- We envision involving 200,000 Metro NYC and global leaders praying through this plan as we cast the vision locally and globally through our US cities and global calls. We will promote this prayer strategy to inform those leaders who will interact with this plan in each year. Movement.org leadership will host and guide these interactions.

Element #2: Multiply Churches

- We will annually assess our efforts with church-planting networks representing denominational and ethnic networks (e.g. Southern Baptists, Assemblies of God, Hope Church Network, Orchard, Conlico, PALM—Chinese) regarding their own church-planting experiences and linking them to the City to City incubator program. We will create a map of current church plants and places where there are communities and regions with a thin presence of life-giving churches.

- We will provide an annual report on the progress of City to City incubator church-planting training. We will promote the vision for 100 church planters annually to start the incubator.

- We will specifically link Revive Long Island church planters with the CTC incubator program with the goal of seeing ten church planters per year from Long Island emerge toward the goal of seeing 100 new church plants by 2030 on Long Island. Revive Long Island will promote this opportunity at every gathering, which meets two to three times a year.

- Tyler Prieb from Church of the City will create multiple stories in a variety of media expressions per year to highlight the innovative work of church planters.

- The marketplace leader/pastor cohort (see plan element #5) will promote a church-planting fund. City to City will direct where funding can be used most strategically. We will research and assess the reinvestment of new churches into future church plants.

- Larry Christensen from Cru will convene a church-planting alliance conversation three times a year to assess the needs and opportunities. The alliance will give specific attention to discover what is happening in minority church-planting networks. We also want to assess the state of church planting in northern New Jersey as well as in southern Connecticut.

We are confident of 100,000 new people as a baseline joining new churches based on the City to City incubator methodology and combining new efforts on Long Island and minority church networks. Our prayer goal is to see 200,000 new people join churches in the region. We believe that as the result of the work groups like Young Life, Thrive Collective, and other high school/university-oriented agencies, we have a great opportunity to attract thousands of next-generation church attendees.

Element #3: Reach and Empower Millennials and Next Generation

We see reaching Millennials and Generation Z through several different efforts:

- *Discipleship:* We plan to enlist 250 churches to use the New City Catechism from Redeemer Presbyterian Church and involve an initial 25,000 people (100 per church) in this app by 2024. We will promote it in our annual gatherings and across social media. We will draw attention to the critical trend in churches that very few young people can describe their faith and why they believe (see chapter 5).
- We will form a collaboration between the Fuller Youth Institute and the Youth Pastors' Fellowship, which LEAD.NYC will facilitate. FYI desires to make New York City a hub of training in its 100,000 US church strategy to train junior high and high school students in discipleship. LEAD.NYC will convene 150 youth leaders to hear from FYI leadership by fall 2020 with the appeal to adopt this curriculum by January 2021. We believe that 100 churches can be added per year 2022–2030 to involve 1,000 churches and hit the 1 percent national threshold for the plan by 2030.

We envision this impacting 50,000 young people over the course of a decade. FYI and LEAD.NYC will create a rollout plan by September 2020, and a working group, created in September, will oversee this strategy going forward. FYI and their disciple-ship tools will be integrated into the rhythm of the Youth Pastors' Fellowship, which meets three times per year. The Youth Pastors' Fellowship will enlist three churches each in their respective net-works every year to grow the engaged network.

- *Planting high school campus work:* Young Life has a plan to grow their engagement with young people to 100,000 by 2026. Our plan is to make connections between our New York City church network and Young Life to steer young people toward Young Life in their present cam-pus engagement. The Youth Leaders Network will be an important point of entry. Young Life hosts a January Leaders' Summit, which LEAD.NYC sponsors, and will drive the Youth Leaders Network to send young leaders. Young Life has a new opportunity to plant chapters with new schools, based on the NYC public school ruling not to offer after-school programming in the 2020–2021 school year.

  Young Life is attractive to public schools because they can provide expertise through staff and volunteers to teach, coach, and mentor. The plan is to create a map of opportunity across the fifty-nine community districts and invite volunteers to fill those opportunities and to contribute expertise, strategic acumen, and philan-thropy. Young Life also has a plan to offer part-time youth pastors to join Young Life staff to connect local churches to local schools.

  Thrive Collective has a parallel strategy to Young Life to be present on 540 campuses by 2030. Thrive Col-lective has impacted 50,000 students from 200 schools since 2008. The extrapolation of their history suggests that their programming can influence and reach another 100,000 students. The 2030 plan requires careful coordination between the efforts of Young Life, Thrive Collective, and like-minded churches. The plan is to increase the volunteer pool from 500 to 1,500 volunteers over the course of the decade. Young Life and Thrive Collective leadership will interact on a biweekly basis to coordinate opportunities with the after-school programming mentioned above.

- *Planting university campus work:* InterVarsity is expanding its leadership on campus in New York City from one area to four areas. They currently work with 600 university students. This plan will allow them to give more leadership resources to plant new campus chapters. They also have momentum through the Every Campus movement to start chapters on every campus in the United States. In New York City, the agencies working on campus will have prayer walked every campus by 2021. The plan is also to do an assessment, by 2021, on the state of campus penetration in New York City with the major agencies working on each campus.

- *Mentoring youth:* As a follow-up to students who have interacted with either Young Life or through Thrive Collective, Living Redemption and Praxis offer mentoring programs and skill development. The strategy is to take this large pipeline of young people and point them toward future opportunities. Living Redemption currently mentors 300 students. The vision is to see 5 percent of the emerging students in Young Life and Thrive Collective gain access to additional opportunities. This represents 10,000 students receiving assistance.

Given the starting point of 300 students, we will need to develop a strategy to scale. The initial plan is to invite Living Redemption leadership to participate in the 2020–2021 Advance Leadership Initiative to craft a ten-year plan that can serve 10,000 students by 2030.

- *Students on mission:* The vision is to challenge 10 percent of every youth group in Metro New York City to participate in a summer mission by 2030. The plan is to launch a survey in the 2020–2021 school year through the Youth Leaders' Fellowship to assess how churches are currently doing. Once we have a baseline, we can develop a plan with a measurable goal for the region. We will actively promote the organizations East West and Touch the World, as mentioned in chapter 5.

- *Working team:* Al Miyashta from The Navigators will lead a working team that gathers quarterly to assess the progress against goals to update and populate the dashboard.

- *Funding:* We will invite the marketplace/pastor cohort to consider a decadal funding pool by 2021 to plant new works on NYC campuses under the leadership of Craig Sider.

Collectively we believe that 275,000 young people can be reached and influenced through joint discipleship strategies and by reaching new students in campus settings.

Element #4: Impact the Margins

Given the robust activity of multiple agencies, our plan is primarily to educate and advocate for larger and deeper engagement with the faith/civic community. We will do that in the following ways:

- *Caring for the homeless:* The Bowery Mission currently serves 400,000 meals per year and houses 150 men in sleeping arrangements. Their influence reaches 3,000 people annually, 30,000 over the course of a decade. A new initiative is to have five volunteers from 150 churches adopt each Bowery graduate every year (150 graduates), which involves 750 volunteers a year (9,000 people over a decade). We will enlist the 150 new churches through introductions made at Movement Day and the Pastors' Prayer Summit and spotlighting volunteer opportunities. Ed Morgan is writing an article to coach churches on ways to integrate the poor into the life of our churches by 2021.

  A partner agency is New York City Relief, a mobile feeding unit that also provides aftercare for their clients. They currently have 38,000 interactions per year with homeless people, including offering food security, clothing, and prayer. Our plan is to provide advocacy and awareness for their efforts in this post-COVID environment. As their CEO, Juan Galloway said, "During COVID, we were told to go home. The homeless had no home to go to. The demand for our services has skyrocketed with people lining up around the block to receive what we offer."[4]

- *At-risk youth:* Danny Sanabria from Youth for Christ (see chapter 6) created a plan to enlist 100 churches to generate 1,000 volunteers to mentor at-risk youth in juvenile centers. He has a short list of fifty pastoral friends he is contacting through one-on-one meeting to recruit the first volunteer pool. The 10 Zip Codes Project, which LEAD.NYC is leading, will provide, along with churches, ambassadorial connections into communities to provide volunteers. They have written a proposal to connect 1,000 young people to technology resources in Washington Heights, Manhattan, and East New York, Brooklyn. The proposal focuses on youth without access to the internet who will fall behind educationally because of schools being shut down. The proposal connects local churches as meeting places with technology resources (laptops) and access to mentors with curriculum provided by Young Life.

- *Affordable housing:* The Christian Cultural Center is establishing 2,100 units of affordable housing by 2030, which will assist 8,400 people. This will represent a best practice in a community impacted by gentrification. The plan is to have CCC's pastor A. R. Bernard train 100 area leaders in the art of housing development for the region.
- *Pregnancy counseling:* Avail currently assists 1,000 clients per year with their services. Over the next ten years, Avail's vision is to multiply that number by the thousands, reaching women and men facing unexpected pregnancy or reproductive loss after abortion and at the moment of their decision. By making Avail's support and tools accessible to clients when they need them most, and by mobilizing and equipping churches to respond, Avail will promote a Christian community that will become the first place New Yorkers turn when facing a pregnancy decision. One hundred New York City churches already embrace Avail's nonpolitical Third Way, which will serve as a catalyst and vanguard for transforming the response of the Christian church across the country.

- *Working team:* Ed Morgan will lead the margins-focused working team, who will meet quarterly to assess the progress of their efforts and provide updated data for the dashboard.

We believe this working team and those who will join will be able to reach and influence 250,000 marginalized people. Considering the number of agencies in this ecosystem and the connections through this working group, we believe that is an achievable number.

Element #5: Mobilize the Marketplace

- The 2030 vision is to involve 30,000 Manhattan Christians in a faith-and-work group. This would represent 50 percent of the active Christians participating. The plan involves promoting the availability of existing groups (see roster at end of chapter 7) through our church network under the leadership of Chip Roper at the VOCA Center. Roper will interface with the New Canaan Society leadership, along with visible marketplace Christians (Bob Doll, April Tam Smith, Tom Cole), to create an awareness campaign by 2021 on the opportunities available in Metro New York.
- Chip Roper, in consultation with marketplace Christian leaders, will determine by 2021where there are gaps in the right kind of available faith and work groups. He will put together a plan to map out the birthing of new groups by 2030 that will engage more marketplace Christians. Roper has proposed that a team from the leadership of various faith and work agencies collaborate to cross promote offerings both in person and

digitally. Roper will lead the VOCA Center to assist 1,000 people a year to find employment through their training on job search. Over a decade that will assist 10,000 people.

- Craig Sider, CEO of Movement.org, will shepherd the creation of a marketplace leader/pastor cohort by 2021. This cohort would meet twice annually. Bob Doll has agreed to help lead the group. The vision is to have 100 marketplace leaders who will represent a board of reference to interact with this plan and to make strategic recommendations. Sider will also guide the group into creating a possible fund to assist with strategic initiatives (funding church plants, groups planting new work on high school and university campuses, poverty initiatives).

- Craig Sider will oversee the marketplace working group, who will meet quarterly to assess their plans and updates for the dashboard.

We believe the collective impact of this group could be 100,000 people by 2030. This would happen by participating in faith-and-work groups and by each member influencing three peers in their professional spheres through friendship and engagement in projects.

The Value of Planning

President Eisenhower said, "Plans are worthless, but planning is everything."[5] Why did he say that? In reflecting on the D-Day invasion of June 6, 1944, Eisenhower recognized the importance of investing the necessary time and thought with all the necessary stakeholders to achieve their mission. It was the largest military invasion in world history, carrying with it the objective of defeating the Nazi army. Plans changed once soldiers hit the beach; the objective did not change.

In 2010 we launched The New York City Movement Project with a vision to plant 100 churches, train 20,000 leaders, and establish Movement Day. A decade later we have far surpassed those benchmarks. Movement Day alone has impacted, in a decade, 400 cities and 40,000 leaders.

As we wade into this effort, the plan will change. We invite every stakeholder to add their contribution to the goal, which is to see God work in powerful ways toward a new spiritual awakening with millions of people being drawn to Him in Metro New York City.

2030 Plan On A Page

Reaching and influencing 1 million+ Metro New Yorkers through:

Praying: mobilizing 250,000 faith leaders to engage in daily prayer for this plan

- Daily prayer through pray.nyc 24/7 prayer chain
- Monthly prayer in our monthly gathering
- Quarterly prayer gatherings led by pray.nyc
- Annual gathering at Pastors' Prayer Summit

Multiplying Churches: seeing 200,000+ people come to faith and join churches

- Help populate the City to City incubator with 100+ leaders per year
- Link Revive Long Island and ten church planters per year with CTC incubator
- Assess the strength of other church-planting networks by 2021

Empowering Millennials and the Next Generation: Engaging 275,000+ young people

- Disciple 75,000 young people through FYI curriculum and Redeemer Catechism
- See 100,000 young people engaged in Young Life by 2026
- See 100,000 young people engaged in Thrive Collective from 540 campuses

Serving the Margins: Serving 250,000+ people in poverty

- Scale the current involvement of homeless agencies to 100,000 people through existing agencies
- See 150,000 collectively impacted from affordable housing, zip-code initiatives

Mobilizing the Marketplace: See 100,000 marketplace leaders engaged

- Involve 30,000 people in faith and work groups
- Influence 70,000 through marketplace Christians
- Raise $25 million in philanthropy to fund strategic initiatives

Chapter 9

100 MILLION

Yankee Stadium is on the corner of 161st Street and River Avenue in the Bronx, and it is one of my favorite places to visit. It is the "Cathedral of Baseball" where the New York Yankees play. The Yankees have won twenty-seven world championships, more than any other team in any sport. I have followed the Yankees for more than fifty years, beginning as a young child when I watched Micky Mantle on television.

The capacity of Yankee Stadium is 50,287 seats.[1] I have been there many times when the stadium was full—once when I attended game 3 of the playoffs in 2017 against the Houston Astros. The stadium was electric with energy. There is nothing quite like a full stadium of cheering, delirious fans. Until you read the book of Revelation.

In Revelation 5:11, John the apostle writes, "I looked and heard the voice of many angels, numbering thousands upon thousands, and ten thousand times ten thousand. They encircled the throne and the living creatures and the elders." Ten thousand times 10,000 is 100 million. That is Yankee Stadium times 20,000. Think about that.

History does not end with a pandemic or a world war. History does not end when a military leader pulls a lever to unleash an atomic bomb. History ends in a galactic prayer meeting with 100 million angels and worshipers from every tribe and tongue.

David Bryant, father of the modern-day prayer movement, writes, "Jesus is not only the summation and consummation of Christian hope, He is also the source of profound approximations of that hope poured out on His Church every day, in a host of ways. Whether with a congregation or a whole nation, every God-given revival is a foretaste of the 'Final Revival,' the one awaiting us at the very moment Christ openly returns to reign."[2]

After thirty-five years of life and leadership in New York City, this is what I have come to realize: those of us alive and active in the church of Metro New York City have seen the "approximation of the consummation" with our very eyes. As perhaps the most international church in human history, we have been at prayer, unity, and collaboration for more than three decades. This book—and the 2030 goal we are aiming toward—are a reflection on early signs of this ultimate consummation.

Throughout this book we have reflected on the enormous challenges facing the churches of New York City, the church of the United States, and the global church. It is easy to feel paralyzed and to despair over the daunting nature of these challenges. If we look only with human eyes at the depth and breadth of the work ahead of us, we can certainly feel helpless and overwhelmed.

We have a 2030 vision of what God can do in our great city and region. And I believe we have the passion, talent, and strategic acumen to make an enormous, world-historic difference. Yet without God's intervention through the mystery of personal and united prayer, we are fooling ourselves to think that we are clever enough to make any lasting difference on our own.

Earlier in this book I made three references to prayer: Josh Crossman reminded us of the urgency of the hour given trends of young people leaving the church. Jon Tyson commented on the urgent need for revival as the only hope for the church and Western civilization. And Tim Keller reflected on the impact of hundreds of churches praying every day for Redeemer Presbyterian Church in Manhattan to be successfully planted. If we hope to see 2030 become a reality, then we must ground everything we do in prayer.

Why Pray Above All Else?

The books of Hebrews and 2 Peter remind us that Jesus is the great High Priest who invites us to enter the mystery of His Priesthood as intercessors—which is amazing when you consider who we are. In *Prayer*, Philip Yancey writes, "Consider that if the Milky Way galaxy were the size of the entire continent of North America, our solar system would fit in a coffee cup. Yet this vast neighborhood of our sun—in truth the size of a coffee cup—fits along with several hundred billion others stars and their minions in the Milky Way, one of perhaps 100 billion such galaxies in the universe. To send a light-speed message to the edge of that universe would take 15 billion years."[3] In other words, we are a speck on a speck on planet Earth.

Yet Isaiah 40:26 reminds us to "lift up your eyes and look to the heavens: Who created all these? He who brings out the starry host one by one and calls forth each of them by name. Because of his great power and mighty strength, not one of them is missing."

The God who is mindful of every star in the universe is mindful of us. God wants us to have this perspective as we approach Him in prayer.

The other side of this perspective is our own helplessness. My mother-in-law, June Johnson, gave me O. Hallesby's book *Prayer* in 1979, the year before Marya and I were married. I read the book shortly after our December 1980 wedding, just as I received news that I had just lost my new position with the IRS because of a federal hiring freeze. I had not expected a major life disruption in my third week of marriage.

Hallesby's words struck me like a thunderbolt: "Helplessness is the real secret and the impelling power of prayer. . . . We . . . learn to know Him so well that we feel safe when we have left our difficulties with Him. To know Jesus in this way is a prerequisite of all true prayer."[4]

In that season of vocational uncertainty and helplessness, God used this disruption and time of prayer to lead me in June 1981 to join the staff of InterVarsity. That decision led to my traveling to India, which led to our move to New York City, which led to the eventual planting of Movement Day. It was God who birthed a willingness to go anywhere in the world He would take Marya and me in 1979. It was God who birthed the desire to pray, which led to the fulfillment of that 1979 commitment. We are all on deeply personal journeys with God as He takes those journeys and intersects them with His grander purposes. God as is active today to fulfill his 4,000-year-old promise to Abraham to bless all the nations on earth as He was the day after he spoke to Abraham in Genesis 12.

But alongside helplessness, we can often look at the work and the circumstances and feel overwhelmed. Simply put, life is overwhelming. Every one of us has at least one circumstance that is overwhelming us at any one time. As I think back on the past forty years, three overwhelming moments come to mind.

The first is when I sat on the rooftop of our missions compound in Bihar, India, in July 1984. Living in a state the size of Nebraska with 100 million people who survive under incredible poverty was overwhelming. The sheer sense of spiritual darkness was overwhelming. Visiting Hindu temples and seeing the multiplicity of gods and the spiritual enslavement of nearly a billion people was overwhelming.

In that context we met every Friday to pray between three and nine hours with the mission's team. That was, I found, the antidote to being overwhelmed. The more I prayed—fully entering in, over a long period, in community with other passionate leaders, and asking Jesus to intervene in the lives of 100 million people in one state of India—the more confident and empowered and less overwhelmed I felt.

The second overwhelming situation came in 1988 when Marya and I heard a loud noise while in bed in our Flushing, Queens, neighborhood. We thought it was a firecracker. It was a gunshot. A Chinese couple was showing off an apartment they were purchasing for their son who was engaged to be married. A robber approached them and killed the mother. Ten days later Marya returned home from her night shift at the hospital, where she worked as a nurse. Her eyes met the eyes of the man who fit the description of the murderer. He ran off.

It was in 1988 when we began to bring congregations together in Concerts of Prayer against the backdrop of our very violent city. In our first gathering we invited sixteen churches to pray together, and seventy-five congregations showed up. Within eighteen months that model had spread to seven locations. Over a twenty-year period, 2,000 churches and 250,000 people participated. That was the antidote to the violence of our city. We saw the murder rate decline nearly 500 percent in twenty-five years from 1993–2018 (see chapter 2).

The third overwhelming situation came on the Tuesday morning of September 11, 2001, when our Concerts of Prayer Greater New York board hurried from the fifteenth floor of the Empire State Building to the street level of Fifth Avenue and 34th Street. We saw smoke billowing across Fifth Avenue from the explosion of the World Trade Center two miles south. That night I felt so helpless and overwhelmed, I sat on my couch at home and wept uncontrollably.

The antidote? We deepened our prayer together. In January 2002, we had nearly 400 leaders who came to our annual Pastors' Prayer Summit to pray and fast for three days. We also began to work together collaboratively with one another in new ways. We had local and national partners deeply committed to New York City. I believe that 9/11 created the environment for church planters to get started in New York. A decade of praying and a disaster unlike anything we had experienced created the environment for God to do a new thing. We were overwhelmed and helpless. God had to intervene.

Through those three experiences, I have discovered that the more we are overwhelmed by our circumstances, the more we must posture ourselves to be overwhelmed by God.

When we were in India in 1983, I heard about a lay leader who had developed the discipline of reading the Bible every ninety days. When we moved to New York City that next summer, I participated in that exercise. We were overwhelmed moving to New York City with few contacts and no place to live—and Marya three months pregnant. God was our lifeline. But then I set that discipline aside for twenty-six years.

I resumed that discipline in 2010, as I felt the need to go deeper with God in a new season. We were starting Movement Day, and God was opening opportunities to work with the global Lausanne Movement. I needed a good dose of feeling overwhelmed by God again. The most overwhelmed I am by God in that discipline is day 68, which is when I read Matthew 1, Luke 1, and John 1. After centuries of struggle, silence, and exile, God breaks in. After sixty-seven days of the Old Testament, the gospel is powerful, riveting Good News. J. I. Packer says it best in his chapter on "God Incarnate," in *Knowing God*:

> It is here, in the thing that happened at the first Christmas, that the profoundest and most unfathomable depths of the Christian revelation lie. "The Word was made flesh" (John 1:14); God became man; the divine Son became a Jew; the Almighty appeared on earth as a helpless human baby, unable to do more than lie and stare and wriggle and make noises, needing to be fed and changed and taught to talk like any other child. And there was no illusion or deception in this; the babyhood of the Son of God was a reality. The more you think about, the more staggering it gets. Nothing in fiction is so fantastic as is the truth of the incarnation.[5]

The great paradox of leadership is that the God who overwhelms us with Himself leads us into overwhelming challenges He is calling us to face together. As a corollary, the width of our influence is in proportion to the depth of our intimacy with God individually and as a community. It is in the realm of prayer that God shapes us for the assignment He has for us in the world.

How Must We Pray?

The beauty in the way God has made us is we have unlimited expressions of how we can pray individually and collectively. It is important and powerful that we keep in front of us the challenges that we agree on together.

In February 2002, InterVarsity Press asked me to write a book for the first anniversary of 9/11, called *The Power of a City at Prayer*. In it, I wrote about a range of prayer expressions that have been planted in Metro New York City over the past thirty years and are still applicable today. Here are some of those expressions and how we can use them as we pursue praying into reality 2030.

The Lord's Watch

Patterned after the eighteen-century Moravian movement, 100 Metro NYC churches adopted a day a month, beginning February 1995, to pray for the revival of the church, reconciliation among the races, reformation of society, and evangelistic efforts with the gospel. Any community of thirty churches or agencies can adopt this model with some simple coordination. It is the only possible expression of sustained unity. Every other unity expression will be an event that comes and goes.

The power of this model is that we have seen God respond in unprecedented ways, both historically and in contemporary times. For the Moravians, they prayed unceasingly for 100 years with the result that 300 missionaries were out from their community to share the Good News with the rest of the world. In *Spiritual Dynamics,* Richard Lovelace said that the Moravian prayer movement was the most vibrant expression of Christianity since the early church.[6]

The closest current expression of this effort is what Jon Tyson's congregation is leading at Church of the City. They have birthed pray.nyc as a 24/7 prayer model for the city. Our invitation is to invite everyone in our sphere of influence to recommit to a daily prayer rhythm over the ambitions of our 2030 decadal vision for Metro New York City.

Concerts of Prayer for Congregations

Many congregations faithfully meet every National Day of Prayer on the first Thursday of May. The National Day of Prayer was constituted by President Truman in 1952. In this Concerts of Prayer model, we see typically three aspects of praying: *adoration* as a worship theme; *awakening* with emphasis on praying for unity and spiritual vitality of the church; and *advance* with its emphasis on the outreach of the church spiritually and socially. We have seen as many as twenty-five simultaneous Concerts of Prayer in our region on the National Day of Prayer.

A current expression of this in addition to the National Day of Prayer is pray.nyc, which New York City pastors Ejaz Nabie and Joel Sadaphal lead. Hundreds of leaders are gathering online to pray in a coordinated way, especially now emerging from the COVID crisis. The first three online gatherings in 2020 with pray.nyc drew 43,000 participants.

Globally we saw 3,000 leaders gathering on Zoom calls, including the Movement Day Global Leader call in April 2020.

Pray New York!

Every June since 2000, a prayer walk in New York City by zip code has taken place. Churches agree to take time on a Saturday and pray for their community by leaving the building and praying *in* and *through* the community. We have had as many as 8,000 people pray in nearly all NYC's zip codes on the same day. They pray specifically for their community's schools, businesses, neighborhoods, and residents.

Pastors' Prayer Summit

For the past thirty years, pastors and ministry leaders from Metro NYC have met for forty-eight hours at Tuscarora Inn, in the Pocono Mountains. We have had more than 6,000 participants at a single summit. During our time together, we participate together in extended worship, a centered meditation (such as focusing on Psalm 23 or Psalm 127) from which we pray together, shared meals, and celebrating communion. The Prayer Summit was birthed in the 1980s by Dr. Joe Aldrich from Multnomah College.

What we have discovered with the Prayer Summit is that leaders spend more time together over a forty-eight-hour period than they typically do the rest of the year combined. It is often the first time that leaders who come from a particular denominational or ethnic culture experience a fuller expression of the body of Christ. It is one of those ways that God overwhelms us with the beauty and diversity of His church. In Metro New York City, LEAD.NYC is leading this effort under Adam Durso. Durso comes from a strong prayer culture at Christ Tabernacle with its 1,000-person weekly prayer meetings. The Metro NYC Pastors' Prayer Summit has become the largest and most diverse gathering of its type in the nation.

Monthly Leader Prayer

For the past twenty-five years, ten to twenty leaders have been meeting as a leader group the first Thursday of each month in Manhattan at Calvary Baptist to pray together. This has become a nexus for leaders to connect throughout the city and pray corporately. It is a microcosm of the prayer summit.

Individual Fasting and Prayer

One of the extraordinary models for fasting and prayer comes from Christian Union under the leadership of Matt Bennett. It draws on the rich models of fasting in prayer from the lives of Moses, Elijah, Nehemiah, Mordecai, Esther, Ezra, John the Baptist, Jesus, and first-century churches. They describe fasting this way: "Fasting, simply put, is going without food and perhaps liquids for a definitive period of time to humble oneself before God. It is sometimes accompanied by mourning and grieving."[7] God has answered powerfully to this prayer and fasting emphasis with growth across Ivy League campus groups and through planting Christian Union expressions in cities.

As we participate in these different prayer expressions with our eyes on 2030, I invite us to pray that we can influence 1 million or more people in our region with the gospel through our collective efforts. We need to pray specifically for the multiplication of churches.

Can we agree to pray every day for the 1,000 church plants City to City forecasts to come to fruition for the city and region?

Can we agree to pray every day for the 250,000 young people who will be drawn to the work of Young Life, InterVarsity, The Navigators, Cru, Thrive Collective, Living Redemption, and their ecosystem agencies and churches?

Can we agree to pray every day that we will be able to assist and give new life to 250,000 marginalized people through the work of The Bowery, The Rescue Alliance, Hope for New York, Youth for Christ, Avail, and their ecosystem partner agencies?

Can we agree to pray every day that 30,000 Christian marketplace leaders in Manhattan will find their way into a faith and work group? Can we pray with the VOCA Center, Christian Union, New Canaan Society, Generosity NY, and all the ecosystem agencies that we can see this achieved? Can we pray for the formation of a 100-leader cohort of pastors and marketplace leaders to give spiritual leadership to the great challenges of the region?

Can we pray every day that 300 cities globally will adopt this methodology of united prayer toward their own unique decadal vision?

What Is Next?

My hope is that you will recommit yourself to a passionate pursuit of God individually and collectively in your own city. The expression of that passion begins in deepening your devotion expressed through prayer and Scripture. It is as important to do this corporately as it is collectively. This will require a high degree of intention around deepened daily practices.

Second, let us agree on what can happen in our cities as we collectively respond to the challenges we have presented in this book about multiplying churches, impacting the next generation, and caring for the poor. We are responsible to become students and servants of our cities. We can only love that which we know. This book is a starting roadmap for Metro New York City. I am confident that leaders, stories, and initiatives will add to the robustness of this vision over the course of the decade.

Third, we need to give ourselves as generously as we can for the causes before us. Let us make a long-term commitment to the place where God has placed us. The two keys to fruitfulness are longevity and proximity. To impact a city or community, we must be planted there. We must be proximate to those we seek to influence.

We need to invite God to overwhelm us with His Person and His Presence. We are part of that great cloud of witnesses that stretches back to Adam and joins 100 million angels in the galactic prayer meeting at the end of history.

New York City leaders praying at thirtieth Annual Pastors Prayer Summit.

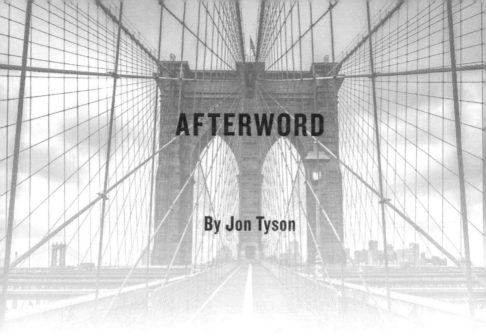

AFTERWORD

By Jon Tyson

One morning I was out praying in Hell's Kitchen, a neighborhood on Manhattan's West Side, at a particularly discouraging season of ministry. Our church had worked so hard with so many initiatives, and had seen only a trickle of the stream we had been praying for. We had sown and watered and labored for what seemed like so little. I was dispirited at the secularity of the city, its godless defiance, and its blatant disregard for the things of God. I stopped under a bridge outside Port Authority with a heavy heart and decided to pray through Romans 1, that great chapter on the power of the gospel. I didn't come to the text with faith, but familiarity, and a sense of helplessness.

Before I got to Romans 1:16 and the power of the gospel, I was struck by something I had never seen before in Romans 1:13: "I do not want you to be unaware, brothers and sisters, that I planned many times to come to you (but have been prevented from doing so until now) in order that I might have a harvest among you, just as I have had among the other Gentiles."

"In order that I may have a harvest among you." Paul was going to Rome for a harvest. This Jewish believer fully expected the gospel of Jesus to reach those outside of his plausibility structure and change them with the Good News. This may seem obvious, but what hit me the most was his vision of gospel movement and response in the global center of empire. Rome seemed like the least likely place the movement of Jesus would take root and flourish. It was only a few decades earlier Rome had crucified Jesus as a failed political rebel. But yet, Paul knew what faith and a message of hope could do. He went with the eyes of faith, not sight.

Rome said Caesar was Lord, but Paul believed God would produce a harvest of new loyalty.

Rome believed in a pantheon of gods, but Paul anticipated a response to the exclusivity of Jesus.

Rome believed in military might, but Paul believed the Suffering Servant would usher in a Kingdom of love.

Rome believed class and power, but Paul believed Jesus would build a new humanity that defied category in the middle of it all.

Paul wanted to go because he knew what the gospel could do. He had seen its power everywhere he had traveled. The seemingly foolish story of a crucified rabbi could cause cultural shame, but if they believed, it could also usher in another Kingdom.

Paul wanted to get to the most pagan place because it was the place of the largest possible harvest. At the time this may have seemed ridiculous. A failed little movement that would become illegal was not a threat to the power of Rome. Yet 300 years later, Rome would bow its knee to Jesus and the harvest would be larger than even Paul could have imagined.

And as I stood under the bridge, I began to sense that same expectation rise in my heart for the city. It was as if this word became alive. Biblical anticipation began to lift my eyes beyond my circumstance and into a place of promise. If Paul believed that, how could I not? I had another 2,000 years of witness and wonder of what the gospel could do from cities and nations around the world.

And then I thought of New York—the city I love and place I have come to call home. Hasn't a similar thing happened here in these last forty years? Hasn't a place that many wrote off as beyond hope and renewal blossomed into the seeds of a gospel movement? Haven't faithful New Yorkers been seeking God for a harvest for decades and now slowly are seeing it come to light? And isn't this happening in cities around the world? Could it be that we too should anticipate a magnificent harvest? Doubling down on the gospel and mission and throwing all we have into what the Spirit is doing in the world seems like the only thing to do in light of what we are seeing.

May we all be stirred by this provocative and prophetic call of anticipation. May the words in this book ignite our faith that we too will push into the mission of God, and with hunger and humility, may we anticipate another great harvest—in your city and ours—so God's glory is put on display in our time.

—Jon Tyson
Senior pastor, Church for the City, Manhattan

ACKNOWLEDGMENTS

With great gratitude to Ginger Kolbaba and David Sluka. Your passion, effort, and skills have made this publication possible. Very special thanks to Sharon Cushing, whose administrative gifts have made this publication possible.

Thanks to the Movement.org board and Movement.org staff team who give themselves so generously to the 500-city vision.

Thanks to Marya for her courage in journeying with me to New York City in 1984.

Thanks to all the friends who allowed me to tell their stories in this book.

Special thanks to Josh Crossman for the groundbreaking work he has done in his essay *The Great Opportunity*. This has created a lot of fresh "North Star" thinking.

Finally, my deepest affection to Movement Day colleagues across five continents. You are the heroes of the story in your own cities.

ABOUT THE AUTHOR

 **Mac Pier** is the founder of Movement. Org. He was instrumental in creating the Movement Day conference (www. movementday.org), which has convened 40,000 leaders from 400 cities. Pier is also the Co-Catalyst for Cities with the Lausanne movement. He has written numerous books including, *A Disruptive Gospel* and *A Disruptive God*. He and his wife, Marya, have three children and five grandchildren.

ABOUT THE AUTHOR

NOTES

Chapter 1: Fruitfulness

1 Nicole Gelinas, "Why the Next Recession Will Be Brutal for NYC," *New York Post,* September 1, 2019, https://nypost.com/2019/09/01/why-the -next-recession-will-be-brutal-for-nyc/.

2 David Goldman, "Worst Year for Jobs Since '45," CNN Money, January 9, 2009, https://money.cnn.com/2009/01/09/news/economy/jobs_december/.

3 Tony Carnes, *Manhattan Center City Evangelical Churches 2009,* Values Research Institute, New York City.

4 "Coronavirus Death Toll," Worldometer, accessed May 12, 2020, https:// www.worldometers.info/coronavirus/coronavirus-death-toll/.

5 Jeffry Bartash, "Great Depression 2020? The Unofficial U.S. Jobless Rate Is at least 20%—or Worse," MarketWatch, May 11, 2020, https://www. marketwatch.com/story/great-depression-2020-the-unofficial-us-job- less-rate-is-at-least-20or-worse-2020-05-08.

6 Timothy Keller, *Center Church: Doing Balanced, Gospel-Centered Minis- try in Your City* (Grand Rapids, MI: Zondervan, 2012), 13. Emphasis in the original.

7 Timothy Keller, *The New York City Movement Project Video,* The NYC Leadership Center, April 2011.

8 Joshua Crossman, *Five Minutes Until Midnight,* Movement Day New York City, Times Square Church, October 25, 2019.

9 Keller, *Center Church*, 54, 340.

10 Ibid., 375.

11 Tim Keller, Redeemer Grace Journal, August 7, 2015, www.redeemer -grace.org.

12 Keller, *Center Church*, 375.

Chapter 2: Disrupted

1 "Number of Deaths Due to Coronavirus (COVID-19) in New York State as of May 11, 2020, by County," Statista, accessed May 16, 2020, https://www.statista.com/statistics/1109403/coronavirus-covid19-death-number-new-york-by-county/.

2 "World/Countries/Germany," May 18, 2020, worldometers.info.

3 Marina Villeneuve and Lori Hinnant, "NYC Coronavirus Deaths Outnumber 9/11 Death Toll," *Boston Globe*, April 7, 2020, https://www.bostonglobe.com/2020/04/07/nation/nyc-coronavirus-deaths-outnumber-911-toll-ground-zero/.

4 David Mosher, "NYC Will Bury Unclaimed Bodies on a Remote Island after Fourteen Days," BusinessInsider.com, April 9, 2020, https://www.businessinsider.com/nyc-coronavirus-covid-19-hart-island-pottersfield-city-cemetery-burials-2020-4.

5 Mac Pier, *Metro NYC Church Attendance Survey*, May 12, 2020.

6 "Disasters: New York City (NYC): The Great Fire of 1776," NYCdata, accessed May 16, 2020, https://www.baruch.cuny.edu/nycdata/disasters/fires-1776.html.

7 Robert Carle, *Sings of Hope in the City* (Valley Forge, PA: Judson Press, 1997), 30.

8 Ed Stetzer, "Fulton Street Revival Anniversary," *Christianity Today*, September 23, 2007, https://www.christianitytoday.com/edstetzer/2007/september/fulton-street-revival-anniversary.html.

9 Kathryn Long, *The Revival of 1857–1858* (New York: Oxford Press, 1998), 48.

10 "1860," BiggestUSCities.com.

11 "Total Population by Census Tract, New York City, 1920," accessed May 16, 2020, https://www1.nyc.gov/assets/planning/download/pdf/data-maps/nyc-population/historical-population/1920_total_pop.pdf.

12 "Statistics: Countries Where the Salvation Army Is Officially at Work," The Salvation Army International, accessed May 16, 2020, https://www.salvationarmy.org/ihq/statistics.

13 Norris Magnuson, *Salvation in the Slums* (Grand Rapids, MI: Baker Publishing, 1990), 16–17.

14 Dana L. Robert, "Simpson, Albert Benjamin (1843–1919): Founder of the Christian and Missionary Alliance," Boston University School of Theology, History of Missiology, accessed May 16, 2020, http://www.bu.edu/missiology/missionary-biography/r-s/simpson-albert-benjamin-1843-1919/.

15 Magnuson, *Salvation*, 17.

16 Joyce Mendelsohn, *The Lower East Side Remembered and Revisited* (New York: Columbia University Press, 2009), 261.

17 Magnuson, *Salvation*, 50.

18 Joshua Crossman, *The Great Opportunity* (Seattle, WA: Pinetops Foundation, 2018), 37–38, www.thegreatopportunity.org.

19 Carl Ellis, *Beyond Liberation* (Downers Grove, IL: InterVarsity Press, 1983).

20 Lesley Kennedy, "Most Immigrants Arriving at Ellis Island in 1907 Were Processed in a Few Hours," history.com, March 7, 2019, https://www.history.com/news/immigrants-ellis-island-short-processing-time.

21 Joseph Berger, "Aided by Orthodox, City's Jewish Population Is Growing Again," *New York Times*, June 11, 2012, https://www.nytimes.com/2012/06/12/nyregion/new-yorks-jewish-population-is-growing-again.html.

22 Curtis Mitchell, *God in the Garden* (Garden City, NY: Doubleday, 1957), 9–10.

23 "Evangelism: 250,000 Hear Graham in New York's Central Park," *Christianity Today*, October 28, 1991, https://www.christianitytoday.com/ct/1991/october-28/evangelism-250000-hear-graham-in-new-yorks-central-park.html.

24 Andrea Elliott, "Political Conversion of New York's Evangelicals," *New York Times*, November 14, 2004, https://www.nytimes.com/2004/11/14/nyregion/the-political-conversion-of-new-yorks-evangelicals.html.

25 History.com Editors, "Ford to City: Drop Dead," History.com, accessed May 16, 2020, https://www.history.com/topics/us-states/ford-to-city-drop-dead-video.

26 Joe Flood, "Why the Bronx Burned," *New York Post*, May 16, 2010, https://nypost.com/2010/05/16/why-the-bronx-burned/.

27 Deonna S. Turner, "Crack Epidemic: United States History (1980s)," *Encyclopedia Britannica*, accessed May 16, 2020, https://www.britannica.com/topic/crack-epidemic/.

28 "New York Crime Rates 1960–2018," disastercenter.com.

Chapter 3: The Great Opportunity

1   "The National Study of Youth and Religion in a Nutshell," 2011, 3, http://assets.ngin.com/attachments/document/0042/5177/NationalStudyYout_Religion.pdf.

2   Joshua Crossman, *The Great Opportunity* (Seattle, WA: Pinetops Foundation, 2018), 58, www.thegreatopportunity.org.

3   Ibid., 22, 10.

4   Ibid., 23.

5   Khary Bridgewater, DeVos Foundation, May 7, 2020.

6   Crossman, *Great Opportunity*, 5, 16, 22.

7   Ibid., 32.

8   Ibid., 42.

9   "US Population 2020," worldometers.info; "NYC Metro Area Population 1950–2020," macrotrends.net.

10 Crossman, *Great Opportunity*, 58.

11 Ibid., 62–65.

12 Ibid., 77–78.

13 Carey Nieuwhof, "Half of All Churches Are Instantly Growing. Here's Why and What to Do," April 2020, https://careynieuwhof.com/half-of -all-churches-are-instantly-growing-heres-why-and-heres-what-to-do/.

14 Department of Labor, "April Job Losses Highlight the Depth of the Pandemic's Devastation," *New York Times*, May 8, 2020, https://www. nytimes.com/2020/05/08/business/stock-market-coronavirus-jobs -report.html#link-7634dae.

15 Kristin Schwab, "Food Pantries Struggle to Provide during COVID 19," Marketplace.org, March 31, 2020, https://www.marketplace. org/2020/03/31/covid-19-food-pantries/.

16 Sara Aridi, "Facing Food Insecurity on the Front Lines," *New York Times*, May 6, 2020, https://www.nytimes.com/2020/04/10/neediest-cases /feeding-america-food-banks-coronavirus.html.

17 "Food Bank for New York: Fiscal Year 2018," foodbanknyc.org.

18 Crossman, *Great Opportunity*, 107.

19 Ibid., 101.

20 Ibid., 112–115.

Chapter 4: Multiply

1   Tony Carnes, *Manhattan Church Planting Report*, Values Research Insti- tute, 2014.

2   Interview with Jon Tyson and Robert Guerrero, May 5, 2020. Interview has been edited for clarity and length.

3   From personal interview with Drew Hyun, April 17, 2020.

4   Mac Pier, *Consequential Leadership* (Downers Grove, IL: InterVarsity Press, 2012), 31.

5   Redeemer City to City Incubator, www.citytocity.nyc.

NOTES

6   Jon Tyson, "Seeking God for Revival," Pastor's Prayer Summit, Tuscarora Inn, Mount Bethel, Pennsylvania, January 28, 2020.
7   Vision statement, pray.nyc.
8   "Elmhurst Fact, NYC Health + Hospitals/Elmhurst," www.nychealth andhopitals.org.

Chapter 5: Next

1   Michael Dimock, "Defining Generations: Where Millennials End and Gen Z Begins," Pew Research Center, January 17, 2019, https://www.pewresearch.org/fact-tank/2019/01/17/where-millennials-end-and-generation-z-begins/.
2   David Kinnaman and Mark Matlock, *Faith for Exiles* (Grand Rapids, MI: Baker Publishing, 2019), 19.
3   Luke Greenwood, *Global Youth Culture* (Eden Prairie, MN: Steiger International, 2019), 18.
4   Ibid., 36–39.
5   Al Miyashita, *Millennial Working Group Report* (New York: Co-Lab, April 2020), 1.
6   Ibid., 5.
7   Greenwood, *Global Youth Culture*, 74.
8   From personal interview with Jeremy Del Rio, March 24, 2020.
9   Miyashta, *Millennial Working Group*, 12.
10 Kinnaman and Matlock, *Faith for Exiles*, 11.
11 Ibid., 54.
12 *The New City Catechism Devotional*, newcitycatechism.com.
13 Kinnaman and Matlock, *Faith for Exiles*, 93.
14 "2018–2019 School Diversity in New York City, 2018-2019 School Year," connect.nyc.gov.

Chapter 6: Margins

1   Jonathan Kozol, *Amazing Grace* (New York: Random House, 1995), 1.
2   Interview with Chris Whitford, April 9, 2020.
3   Joshua Crossman, *The Great Opportunity* (Seattle, WA: Pinetops Foundation, 2018), 81, www.thegreatopportunity.org.
4   "New York City Population 2020," usapopulation.org.
5   "The New York City Government Poverty Measure 2005–2017," The Mayor's Office for Economic Opportunity: Poverty Measure-Opportunity," https://www1.nyc.gov/site/opportunity/poverty-in-nyc/poverty-measure.page.

6   Roger Scotland, *Signs of Hope in the City* (Valley Forge, PA: Judson Press, 1997), 157–158.

7   "We Have Hope for New York," Hope for New York, https://www.hfny.org/about.

8   "History," Rescue Alliance, https://www.rescuealliance.nyc/history.

9   Ibid.

10 Brandon Vogt, "Jesus in His Most Distressing Disguise," *Word on Fire*, September 5, 2014, https://www.wordonfire.org/resources/blog/jesus-in-his-most-distressing-disguise/20850/.

11 Interview with Ed Morgan, April 2, 2020.

Chapter 7: Marketplace

1   Mac Pier, *Spiritual Life in the Global City* (Birmingham, AL: New Hope, 2008), 33.

2   "Why Gotham?" Center for Faith and Work, http://faithandwork.com/programs/1-gotham-fellowship.

3   *New York City: The Heart of Cultural Influence*, Christian Union, https://www.christianunion.org/ministries/cities/new-york-city.

4   Joshua Crossman, *The Great Opportunity* (Seattle, WA: Pinetops Foundation, 2018), 106, www.thegreatopportunity.org.

5   *Help Mobilize Prayer & Gospel Communities on Every Campus*, Every Campus, https://everycampus.com/.

6   Mitchell Moss and Carson Qing, *The Dynamic Population of Manhattan*, Wagner School of Public Service, New York University, March 1, 2012, https://wagner.nyu.edu/impact/research/publications/dynamic-population-manhattan.

Chapter 8: 2030

1   Shiloh Turner, Kathy Merchant, John Kania, and Ellen Martin, "Understanding the Value of Backbone Organizations in Collective Impact: Part 1," *Stanford Social Innovation Review*, July 17, 2012, https://ssir.org/articles/entry/understanding_the_value_of_backbone_organizations_in_collective_impact_1.

2   Interview with Juan Galloway, June 5, 2020.

3   Shiloh Turner, et al, "Understanding the Value of Backbone Organizations."

4   Interview with Juan Galloway, June 5, 2020.

5   Dwight D Eisenhower, "Remarks at the National Defense Executive Reserve Conference," The American Presidency Project,

November 14, 1957, https://www.presidency.ucsb.edu/documents/
remarks-the-national-defense-executive-reserve-conference.

Chapter 9: 100 Million

1   Ben Shpigal, "Vazquez's Final Pitch in Pinstripes?," *New York Times*,
    October 14, 2010, https://www.nytimes.com/2010/10/14/sports/baseball
    /14juice.html.

2   David Bryant, "What Does It Look Like When Christ Rules a People
    through Revival?," December 7, 2016, https://christnow.com/what-does
    -it-look-like-when-christ-rules-a-people-through-revival/.

3   Philip Yancey, *Prayer* (Grand Rapids, MI: Zondervan, 2006), 20.

4   O. Hallesby, *Prayer* (Minneapolis, MN: Augsburg, 1931, 1959, 1994),
    23, 48.

5   J. I. Packer, *Knowing God* (Downers Grove, IL: InterVarsity Press,
    1973), 46.

6   Mac Pier, *The Power of a City at Prayer* (Downers Grove, IL: InterVarsity
    Press, 2002), 77–78.

7   "About Fasting," Christian Union, https://www.christianunion.org/new
    /84-get-involved/40-days-of-prayer-fasting/1435-about-the-initiative.